The Dionysian Mystical Theology

The Dionysian Mystical Theology

Paul Rorem

Fortress Press
Minneapolis

THE DIONYSIAN MYSTICAL THEOLOGY

Cover image: St. Dionysius the Areopagite, © Filippos Konstantaras, logicon.deviantart.com/

Cover design: Tory Herman

Library of Congress Cataloging-in-Publication Data

Print ISBN: 978-1-4514-9582-9

eBook ISBN: 978-1-5064-0044-0

The paper used in this publication meets the minimum requirements of American National Standard for Information Sciences — Permanence of Paper for Printed Library Materials, ANSI Z329.48-1984.

Manufactured in the U.S.A.

This book was produced using PressBooks.com, and PDF rendering was done by PrinceXML.

Contents

Part II. Stages of Dionysian Reception and Interpretation

Mapping the Tradition Series

Paul Rorem, series advisor

Mapping the Tradition is a series of brief, compact guides to pivotal thinkers in Christian history. Each volume focuses upon a particular figure and provides a concise but lucid introduction to the central features of each author's work and sketches the lasting significance of that thinker for the history of Christian theology. As well, the series utilizes primary source works from each figure as an entry point for exposition and exploration. Guided by leading scholars in history and theology, primary source texts are reproduced with explanatory commentary, and are accompanied by orientational essays to the context, contours, and historical and conceptual legacy of the corpus. This series is designed for beginning and intermediate students, as well as interested general readers, who will benefit from clear, helpful surveys of thinkers, texts, and theologies from across the epochs of Christian history and introduction to major issues and key historical and intellectual points of development.

Forthcoming volumes in the series include:

Gillian T. W. Ahlgren, *Enkindling Love: The Legacy of Teresa of Avila and John of the Cross*

Khaled Anatolios, *Irenaeus of Lyons: The Making of the Great Tradition*

Romanus Cessario, O.P. and Cajetan Cuddy, O.P., *Thomas and the Thomists: The Achievement of Thomas Aquinas and his Interpreters*

Robert Kolb, *Luther and Christian Freedom*

Andrew Louth, *John of Damascus: The Radiance of Orthodoxy*

Paul R. Sponheim, *Existing Before God: Søren Kierkegaard and the Human Venture*

Terrence N. Tice, *Schleiermacher: The Psychology of Christian Faith and Life*

Thomas G. Weinandy and Daniel A. Keating, *Athanasius: Trinitarian-Incarnational Soteriology and Its Reception*

Abbreviations

The Mystical Theology and other works by Pseudo-Dionysius will be cited according to three editions, using the usual abbreviations:

MT *The Mystical Theology*

DN *The Divine Names*

CH *The Celestial Hierarchy*

EH *The Ecclesiastical Hierarchy*

Ep The Letters

First will be the traditional location in Migne (*Patrologia Cursus Completus, Series Graeca*, volume 3), then the critical edition (*Corpus Dionysiacum, Patristische Texte und Studien*, volume 33 for *The Divine Names* and volume 36 for all other Dionysian works [Berlin: de Gruyter, 1990–1991]), and finally the page number in *Pseudo-Dionysius: The Complete Works*, translated by C. Luibheid (New York: Paulist, 1987).

Biblical passages are cited and abbreviated according to the New Revised Standard Version.

Biblical and Liturgical Symbols	Paul Rorem, *Biblical and Liturgical Symbols within the Pseudo-Dionysian Synthesis* (Toronto: Pontifical Institute of Mediaeval Studies, 1984).
Commentary	Paul Rorem, *Pseudo-Dionysius: A Commentary on the Texts and an Introduction to Their Influence* (New York: Oxford University Press, 1993).
Scholia	Paul Rorem and John Lamoreaux, *John of Scythopolis and the Dionysian Corpus: Annotating the Areopagite* (Oxford: Clarendon, 1998).
Eriugena's Commentary	Paul Rorem, *Eriugena's Commentary on the Dionysian Celestial Hierarchy* (Toronto: Pontifical Institute of Mediaeval Studies, 2005).
Hugh of St. Victor	Paul Rorem, *Hugh of St. Victor* (New York: Oxford University Press, 2009).

Publication Data

The following publishers are acknowledged for their permission to reproduce material in this book.

"The Doctrinal Concerns of the First Dionysian Scholiast, John of Scythopolis," in *Denys l'Aréopagite et sa postérité en Orient et en Occident*, ed. Ysabel de Andia (Paris: Études Augustiniennes, 1997), 187-200. © Institut d'Études Augustiniennes, by permission.

"The Early Latin Dionysius: Eriugena and Hugh of St. Victor," in *Modern Theology* 24:4 (2008): 601-614. Also published in *Re-thinking Dionysius the Areopagite*, ed. Sarah Coakley and Charles Stang (Oxford: Blackwell, 2009), 71-84. © the author.

"Martin Luther's Christocentric Critique of Pseudo-Dionysian Spirituality," in *Lutheran Quarterly* 11 (Autumn, 1997): 291-307. © *Lutheran Quarterly*, by permission.

"Negative Theologies and the Cross," in *Harvard Theological Review* 101: 3-4 (2008): 451-464; reprinted in *Lutheran Quarterly* 23 (2009): 314-331. © *Lutheran Quarterly*, by permission.

Quotation of *The Mystical Theology* in full is by permission of Paulist Press, from *Pseudo-Dionysius: The Complete Works*, Translation by

Preface

The double goal of this short book is to introduce the sixth-century Pseudo-Dionysian "mystical theology" and to offer glimpses at key stages in its interpretation and critical reception through the centuries. In part 1, the elusive Areopagite's own miniature essay, *The Mystical Theology*, will be quoted in its entirety, sentence by sentence (courtesy of Paulist Press) with commentary. Yet its cryptic contents would be almost impenetrable without reference to the rest of the Dionysian corpus: *The Divine Names*, *The Celestial Hierarchy*, *The Ecclesiastical Hierarchy*, and the (ten) Letters. While all of these works deserve extensive comments in their own right, and have indeed received such commentary, including my own, they will here be invoked more specifically to shed light on the compressed wording of *The Mystical Theology*. Of special importance in this context is the Dionysian use of negations in an "apophatic" theology that recognizes the transcendence of God beyond human words and concepts.

Stages in the reception and critique of this corpus and theme are sketched in part 2: first, the initial sixth-century introduction and marginal comments or scholia by John of Scythopolis; second, the early Latin translation and commentary by the ninth-century Carolingian theologian Eriugena and the twelfth-century commentary by the Parisian Hugh of St. Victor; and third, the critical reaction by Martin Luther in the sixteenth-century Reformation. In conclusion, the Dionysian apophatic will be presented alongside other forms of negative theology from the Christian tradition in light of modern (and postmodern) interest in the subject.

My comments on *The Mystical Theology* constitute a wholly new composition, but the four essays in part 2 have already been published separately, as itemized in the publication data. With thanks to those original editors and publishers, they are here lightly adjusted and joined together for a sequential narrative. For much more on various stages of the Dionysian reception, see *Re-thinking Dionysius the Areopagite*, edited by Sarah Coakley and Charles M. Stang (Malden, MA: Wiley-Blackwell, 2009), originally published as *Modern Theology* 24, no. 4 (2008).

I am delighted that this slender volume will lead off a new Fortress series, *Mapping the Tradition*, so that other theologians from the Christian tradition can be briefly introduced and have their own reception histories sketched.

For help on this volume, I thank Marcia Tucker, librarian at the Institute for Advanced Study; Michael Gibson, supportive editor at Fortress Press; Judith Attride, patient transcriber; Mark Dixon, research assistant, especially for the apparatus; and Kate Skrebutenas, the library's Director of Access, Research and Outreach at Princeton Theological Seminary and truly my better half.

PART I

An Introduction to Pseudo-Dionysius by Way of *The Mystical Theology*

Preamble

Brief as it is, the Dionysian *Mystical Theology* sometimes yields glimmers of its meaning in short phrases or even individual words, starting with "Dionysius," "mystical," and "theology." Although the proper name "Dionysius" does not appear within *The Mystical Theology* itself, some manuscripts have it in a longer title; furthermore, the personal name is clearly attested not only in the other titles but also within the text elsewhere.[1] To take a prime example, the first treatise in this corpus (according to the overwhelming manuscript evidence) begins this way: "Dionysius the Presbyter to Timothy the Co-Presbyter, Concerning the Celestial Hierarchy."[2] Leaving "Timothy" aside for the moment, since that name makes its own appearance within *The Mystical Theology* shortly, as do the two major terms in the title, we start with "Dionysius" himself, the purported author.

In the Acts of the Apostles, when the apostle Paul finds himself in Athens, the narrative and his speech both make explicit reference to the city's philosophical traditions. Epicureans and Stoics are named (17:18), a Stoic poet (Aratus) is quoted by Paul as writing "For we are indeed his offspring" (17:28b), allusions are made to Pythagoras,

1. Ep 7, 1081C, 170.4, 269. For the system of Dionysian citations, see the abbreviations in the front matter.
2. CH 1, 120A, 7.1–2, 145.

Plato, and Epictetus,[3] and the enigmatic comment, "In him we live and move and have our being" (17:28a) is expressed. Athenian philosophy is here taken up into Christian eloquence for a purpose, and with a key starting point. Building on his hearers' piety and wanting to bring them further into the truth as he knew it, Paul says that he noticed an altar inscription: "To an unknown god" (17:23). This exact Greek wording becomes crucial. Paul's sermon prompts some scoffing, and he left the Athenians; "But some of them joined him and became believers, including Dionysius the Areopagite and a woman named Damaris, and others among them" (17:34). "Dionysius the Areopagite," one of the few to believe Paul's proclamation that this God who made everything has raised his appointed one from the dead, enters Christian history. Specifically, his name here provided the entrée for a later author to use this exact language of the "unknown" God to trigger a complex concept of "unknowing" and indeed this treatise and entire corpus. Whether Paul gave this speech at the geographical hill or the judicial council of the Areopagus in Athens, the designation of Dionysius as "the Areopagite" points to his important standing in that civic court. (And, whether "Damaris," who was converted with him, is named as his wife or simply "a woman" is another question.)

Acts 17 thus supplies the biblical hook for this treatise and this corpus, not only in the naming of Dionysius but also in the naming of God as "unknown." No wonder that a later author who wanted to adopt Greek philosophical traditions and bend them to Christian readers would choose this name. Early in the sixth century, these "Dionysian" writings suddenly surface, and they were quickly accepted as authentic—that is, from the first century; yet, who really wrote them has never been convincingly established. From 1895,

3. Charles M. Stang, *Apophasis and Pseudonymity in Dionysius the Areopagite* (Oxford: Oxford University Press, 2012), 146.

when the pseudonymity was proven, to the mid-twentieth century, many names were proposed, but none has stuck.[4] The quest remains irresistible, however, as seen recently in the renominations of several contenders. A modern scholar's argument for Dionysian authorship usually matches his or her core convictions. Was our author fundamentally a pagan Neoplatonist, such as Damascius, and not a Christian at all?[5] Or, was he a Syrian Christian like Sergius of Rashaina,[6] or perhaps an educated monk like Peter the Iberian?[7] For our purposes, more important than authorial speculation is the biblical linkage to Paul in Athens. Paul started with Greek philosophy and expanded it into a Christian presentation there, and our "Dionysius" is doing that here as well.[8]

The full title of this little essay could be rendered "To Timothy, regarding Mystical Theology," but the wording calls for immediate clarification. "Timothy," named a "friend" shortly, is called "my son" at the start and end of another treatise,[9] which required of the earliest commentators the creative explanation that the author Dionysius, like Paul himself, was Timothy's elder and spiritual mentor.[10] (The first

4. For the earlier but still useful tabulation of hypotheses about authorship, see Ronald F. Hathaway, *Hierarchy and the Definition of Order in the Letters of Pseudo-Dionysius* (The Hague: M. Nijhoff, 1969), 31–35.
5. C. M. Mazzuchi, "Damascio, autore de Corpus Dionysiacum . . ." *Aevum* 80 (2006): 299–334; see now the refutation by Giocchino Curiello, "Pseudo-Dionysius and Damascius: An Impossible Identification," *Dionysius* 31 (2013): 101–16.
6. Rosemary A. Arthur, *Pseudo-Dionysius as Polemicist* (Aldershot: Ashgate, 2008), 197, building on 119–21, 138, and 184–87. For more on Sergius, see Istvan Perczel, for example, "The Earliest Syriac Reception of Dionysius," *Modern Theology* 24, no. 4 (2008): 557–71, which also appears in *Re-thinking Dionysius the Areopagite*, ed. Sarah Coakley and Charles M. Stang (Oxford: Wiley-Blackwell, 2009), 27–41.
7. Alexander Golitzin, *Mystagogy: A Monastic Reading of Dionysius Areopagita*, ed. Bogdan G. Bucur (Collegeville, MN: Liturgical Press, 2013), 399–406. To be fair, Golitzin's substantial presentations of Dionysius as a (monastic) Christian do not depend on an authorial identification.
8. For more examples of Pauline linkages outside this one treatise, see Stang, *Apophasis,* esp. ch. 3, 81–116.
9. EH 1 369A, 63.3, 195; EH 7 568D, 131.30, 259.
10. *Scholia* 48.7, 154; discussed on 101–02 John's larger doctrinal concerns are presented in part 2 below.

such commentator, or "scholiast," John of Scythopolis, is presented at the start of part 2 below.) Indeed, all four treatises of the Dionysian corpus (*The Celestial Hierarchy*, *The Ecclesiastical Hierarchy*, *The Divine Names*, and *The Mystical Theology*) are presented as spiritual teachings from an experienced leader to a younger man for his development as a leader of others. Often explicit in opening or closing a work, this format is crucial throughout, for this Pauline circle of spiritual guidance then encompasses every reader.

The title itself can be doubly misleading, for our modern ears hear both "mystical" and "theology" far differently than our Greek ancestors—or the earliest translators, for that matter—did. That "mystical" might better be "mysterious" is confirmed by the first extant (Middle) English translation of this word as "hidden."[11] As seen throughout this treatise and corpus, including the "mysteries" or sacraments, the so-called mystical is really something "hidden" or mysterious and yet also now revealed, as the apostle Paul says (Eph. 1:9 and Col. 2:2-3). Only much later did this word family turn into "mysticism" with associations of extraordinary individualistic experiences.[12] Turning an old and dismissive saw on its head, texts like this one do not start in the mist, center on the I, and always end in schism (mist-I-schism) but rather start with Scripture, center on relationships, and usually help to build community. Such, at least, is suggested in this case by the epistolary form of the major works and of course by the ten letters appended: four to "Gaius" (Rom. 16:23 and 1 Cor. 1:14, 3 John), then Dorotheus, Sosipater (Rom. 16:21), Polycarp (of Smyrna?), Demophilus, the Pauline colleague Titus, and, climactically, "John the theologian, apostle and evangelist."[13] These

11. "Denis' Hidden Theology," in *Pursuit of Wisdom and Other Works by the Author of The Cloud of Unknowing*, trans. and ed. James Walsh (New York: Paulist, 1988).
12. See Bernard McGinn, *The Presence of God*, vol. 1, *The Foundations of Mysticism* (New York: Crossroad, 1992), esp. 3–12.
13. Ep 10 1117A, 208.1, 288.

and other personal names from the first century provide both the obvious function of invoking an apostolic milieu and also the more subtle reminder of relationships and spiritual direction as a form of community.

Calling Saint John a "theologian" brings us back to the other potentially misleading word in our title, namely, "theology." As in other early Greek writers, "theo-logy" originally meant "God's word" in the sense of the biblical Scriptures. Examples abound in this treatise and throughout the corpus.[14] Thus, the "theologians" are first of all Scripture writers such as Zechariah, Ezekiel, Isaiah, Peter, and Paul.[15] While "theology" (and theologian) can also expand to mean words and works *about* God, the baseline meaning is biblical. Thus, as we shall see, *The Mystical Theology* really means "God's word, hidden" yet now also revealed. How something of God is both hidden and yet revealed, both known and "unknown," is what the Dionysian affirmations and negations are all about, but cryptically.

14. See the note at MT 1 997A, 133 note 1 and *Biblical and Liturgical Symbols*, 15–18.
15. *Biblical and Liturgical Symbols*, 19.

Chapter One

After the treatise title, we move directly to the body of the text, since the chapter titles added in later manuscripts can be misleading. The text opens, uncharacteristically for Dionysius, with a prayer:

> Trinity!! Higher than any being, any divinity, and goodness! Guide of Christians in the wisdom of heaven! Lead us up beyond unknowing and light, up to the farthest, highest peak of mystic scripture, where the mysteries of God's Word lie simple, absolute and unchangeable in the brilliant darkness of a hidden silence. Amid the deepest shadow they pour overwhelming light on what is most manifest. Amid the wholly unsensed and unseen they completely fill sightless minds with treasures beyond all beauty.[1]

The prayer has a straightforward Christian start ("Trinity," although this too is unusually explicit for Dionysius) but immediately turns cryptic and challenges any reader and every translator. The second word, literally, is "hyperexistent," or "more than existing." That God is existent and yet also beyond existent is a particularly Dionysian form of simultaneous affirmation and negation, all in the prefix *hyper-*. This Greek modifier occurs fully ten times in this opening prayer alone, starting with hyperexistent, hyperdivine, and

1. MT 1 997AB, 141.3–142.4, 135, deleting "our" from "sightless minds." That these "sightless minds" refer to angelic beings is an insight from the scholia of John of Scythopolis. See *Patrologia Graeca* 4:417A, translated as *Scholia* 417.1.

hypergood, all in the opening line. A single prefix here previews and even carries the entire Dionysian "mystical theology" within itself: whatever we think we perceive or know of God, while true on one level, falls short of the transcendent reality, for God is hyper-that, super-that (in the Latin translation), more-than-that. How should such expressions as "superilluminated darkness" or especially "hyperunknown" be translated? Along with this special form of negation, not privation but transcendence, come also other forms of negations, "unsensed and unseen," as in the Pauline "unknown God." That they can continue into double negations ("hyperunknown") does not yield a simple affirmation but a mind-bending, word-stretching challenge to be approached carefully. (At this point, medieval paraphrases add references to "affection beyond the mind," meaning that love progresses beyond knowledge, as presented in part 2 below, but *The Mystical Theology* itself never mentions affection or love.)

Fortunately for the reader, the cryptic prayer to God gives way to direct advice:

> For this I pray; and, Timothy, my friend, my advice to you as you look for a sight of the mysterious things, is to leave behind you everything perceived and understood, everything perceptible and understandable, all that is not and all that is, and, with your understanding laid aside, to strive upward as much as you can toward union with him who is beyond all being and knowledge. By an undivided and absolute abandonment of yourself and everything, shedding all and freed from all, you will be uplifted to the ray of the divine shadow which is above everything that is.[2]

Shifting from his allusive prayer toward the "hyperexistent" God to a direct address to his "friend Timothy," our Dionysius has here previewed the advice of *The Mystical Theology* as a whole and the

2. MT 1 997B–1000A, 142.5–11, 135.

gist of the spiritual direction in his corpus overall. In these few lines, not just "Timothy" but all readers through the centuries are offered a specific form of guidance to the divine in Dionysian terms.[3] The "mysterious" sights, for starters, are "mystical" in the characteristic sense of "hidden," as mentioned above. The way to approach them, says the Areopagite, is to go beyond (to abandon) what is "perceived and understood," a crucial coupling of word families. The perceived or "perceptible" are a matter of the physical sense perceptions, especially what is seen literally or pictured in the mind's eye. Whole treatises present the author's method and examples for understanding what the Scriptures say about the visual appearances of the angels (*The Celestial Hierarchy*) and what the liturgical rites present to the eyes of the worshipper (*The Ecclesiastical Hierarchy*). Knowing how to interpret such perceptible presentations is exactly the (exegetical) process that yields their meanings or concepts—namely, that which is "understood"—in the second half of this compressed coupling. Moving from the biblical or liturgical sense perceptions to the concepts thus understood is the hermeneutical business of those other treatises; here, *The Mystical Theology* presupposes that prior process and abruptly advises the reader(s) to leave behind both the perceptible and also the conceptual or understandable. Negations come in again when going beyond the hard-won concepts of careful thinking, with the recognition, also biblical, that the transcendent God is beyond our realm of sense perception, concepts, and knowledge. That is what *The Mystical Theology* is all about, as apparent in chapter 4 on the perceptible and chapter 5 on the conceptual.

3. The whole Dionysian universe is indeed in this prologue to *The Mystical Theology*. Bruno Forte, "L'universo dionisiano nel prologo della *Mistica teologia*," *Medioevo* 4 (1978): 1–57. Noting parallels and chiasmus in the opening prayer and advice, plus the Latin translations, Forte nicely captures the balance of Dionysian philosophy and spirituality as one unified message.

But this passage has yet more guidance to offer, again with specialized vocabulary. Passing beyond the perceptible and the understandable is a matter of striving "upward . . . toward union" with God. The spatial language of "up" (ana-) pervades the Dionysian vocabulary, sometimes explicitly in terms of "uplifting," as seen shortly. To ascend above our lower realm is not merely an approach to God, however, but fully a "union," he says, with the one beyond all being and knowledge. The advice to Timothy is ambitious indeed, as developed later in this chapter in the account of Moses on Mount Sinai and union with the "unknown" God. Apostolic talk of "union" with God captivated later generations and "mystical theology" in the medieval sense. There is yet more to this opening paragraph of advice, again conveyed in compressed and specialized vocabulary. The "abandonment of yourself and everything" is a form of "ecstasy," literally a "standing outside" of your normal self and its sense perceptions and concepts. Here again, the Dionysian method is a matter of interpreting the perceptible and going beyond the conceptual in a programmatic sequence of spiritual progression, not an "ecstasy" in the casual modern sense, as taken up again below.

To summarize this opening directive, which in fact conveys the overall Dionysian advice: moving above sense perception and the conceptual realm of understanding, "you will be uplifted to the 'superexistent' ray of the divine shadow." The "anagogical" language of uplifting carries shades of hermeneutical tradition and metaphysical background, and it conveys the basic thrust of spiritual uplift. In the Dionysian nomenclature now to be unpacked, this ascent is not simple or generic, but specifically in the challenging terms of apparent contradictions such as "the ray of the divine shadow." What our author makes of light and darkness, rays and shadows, the biblical hiding place (Ps. 18:11) and Sinai's dark cloud (Exod. 20:21) is yet to come.

But First, a Warning

> But see to it that none of this comes to the hearing of the uniformed, that is to say, to those caught up with the things of the world, who imagine that there is nothing beyond instances of individual being and who think that by their own intellectual resources they can have a direct knowledge of him who has made the shadows his hiding place [Ps. 18:11]. And if initiation into the divine is beyond such people, what is to be said of those others, still more uninformed, who describe the transcendent cause of all things in terms derived from the lowest orders of beings, and who claim that it is in no way superior to the godless, multiformed shapes they themselves have made.[4]

Admonitions to literary confidentiality regarding specialized spiritual knowledge were routine in antiquity and common in the Dionysian corpus. The hierarchical treatises, especially, conveyed the caution, again to "Timothy," to share the sacred fittingly and not to throw these pearls before swine.[5] Talk of secrecy and even "swine" may sound extreme, but the point is effectively pedagogical: idolaters need first to be taught a basic truth, and simple believers need to be instructed patiently in the higher truths, rather than explaining everything all at once to everyone. Only the experienced reader is ready for the Areopagite's advanced teaching. "What has actually to be said . . . is this."

Now that Dionysius shifts from a warning about concealment to his main exposition, he introduces directly his (famous) language of affirmations and negations, carefully correlated to God as cause of all and yet also surpassing all. "Since it is the Cause of all beings, we should posit and ascribe to it all the affirmations we make in regard to beings, and, more appropriately, we should negate all these affirmations, since it surpasses all being. Now we should not conclude that the negations are simply the opposites of the affirmations, but

4. MT 1 1000AB, 142.12–143.3, 136.
5. EH 1 372A, 63.7–11, 195. Matt. 7:6; CH2 145C, 17.1–2, 153.

rather that it [the cause of all transcending all] is considerably prior to this, beyond privations, beyond every denial, beyond every assertion."[6]

The nomenclature of affirmations and negations is here explicitly "kataphatic" and "apophatic," respectively. The tradition of "negative" or apophatic theology may not have started with our Dionysius, but from early medieval interpreters through postmodern times it has become closely identified with his contribution to Christian theology. (Varieties of negative theology are surveyed at the end of part 2, below.) Here he carefully correlates affirmations with the "cause of all things," meaning that our warrant for using affirmations about God taken from the realm of beings is that they are all related to God as effects are related to their cause. That God is the cause of all things, in other words, means that we can use all these effects to affirm something about their cause. Yet, and more appropriately, we should negate all of these because God, again, "hyperexists" or exists beyond them all. That God transcends all things, in other words, means that we must negate and thus go beyond any and all such affirmations. In that sense, and following Scripture, we can use negations, but in a specific way and not simply as counterparts of affirmations.

That negations are not just the logical opposites of affirmations signals again the forward or upward thrust of the Dionysian language.[7] Affirmations are possible because all things stem as effects from the "cause of all"; yet, because God transcends all, they must be surpassed like rungs on a ladder by qualifying and thus in a way negating each one. Moreover, since God "surpasses all being," literally, "hyperexists beyond all," God is beyond negations too,

6. MT 1 1000B, 143.3–7, 136.

7. The idea that negations are not just the logical opposites of affirmations is in contrast to Aristotle, *On Interpretation*, 17a.

"beyond every denial." What that might mean is first illustrated biblically.

Bartholomew and Moses

The apostolic age of "the blessed Bartholomew" is invoked to approach this method of affirmation and negation, but cryptically:

> This, at least, is what was taught by the blessed Bartholomew. He says that the Word of God [theo-logy] is vast and miniscule, that the Gospel is wide-ranging and yet restricted. To me it seems that in this he is extraordinarily shrewd, for he has grasped that the good cause of all is both eloquent and taciturn, indeed wordless. It has neither word nor act of understanding, since it is on a plane above all this, and it is made manifest only to those who travel through foul and fair, who pass beyond the summit of every holy ascent, who leave behind them every divine light, every voice, every word from heaven, and who plunge into the darkness [Exod. 20:21] where, as scripture proclaims, there dwells the One who is beyond all things.[8]

Of course, the biblical Bartholomew (Matt. 10, Mark 3, Luke 6) left no such shrewd insights, but his name here helps give Dionysius some authoritative exposition to lead into his main narrative example. The idea that the word of God (theology) is vast, wide-ranging, and eloquent will turn out to apply to affirmations; that it is also miniscule, restricted, and taciturn, even wordless, will apply to negations. Here, the "cause of all" is further characterized as the "good" cause of all, and the biblical source about entering the thick darkness is linked to a (Neo-)Platonic phrase, "the One beyond all things."[9] The forward thrust of this passage is in the verbs of spiritual

8. MT 1 1000BC, 143.8–17, 136. That Dionysius here uses the present tense for what Bartholomew "says" (not "said") supports his apostolic authenticity, according to the comment of John of Scythopolis at PG 4 420AB (*Scholia* 420.2, 244; see discussion on 101.)

9. For this Greek phrase (ὁ πάντων ἐπέκεινα) as part of a hymn from antiquity, see my *Commentary*, p. 42 note 17.

progress: travel, pass beyond, leave behind, plunge into. The stage is set for Moses, Mount Sinai, and a mystical or mysterious cloud.

As the individual advice to Timothy is an essential initial manifesto, so the example of Moses going up Mount Sinai provides the crucial paradigm for Dionysian spiritual ascent. The passage repays rereading for several reasons: the overarching narrative of an upward approach to union with the unknown God, the specialized vocabulary hinting at liturgical experience, and the long and fateful afterlife of its specific phrases in medieval spirituality. We here break the passage into two sections, each quoted in full and then in sequential components. First, the ascent up Mount Sinai:

> It is not for nothing that the blessed Moses is commanded to submit first to purification and then to depart from those who have not undergone this. When every purification is complete, he hears the many-voiced trumpets. He sees the many lights, pure and with rays streaming abundantly. Then, standing apart from the crowds and accompanied by chosen priests, he pushes ahead to the summit of the divine ascents. And yet he does not meet God himself, but contemplates, not him who is invisible, but rather where he dwells. (This means, I presume, that the holiest and highest of the things perceived with the eye of the body or the mind are but the rationale which presupposes all that lies below the Transcendent One. Through them, however, his unimaginable presence is shown, walking the heights of those holy places to which the mind at least can arise.)[10]

By the time our mysterious author crafted this careful itinerary, Moses was a well-traveled prototype for spiritual progress. Gregory of Nyssa, for one prominent example, had interpreted the overall life of Moses in spiritual terms, including his mounting of Sinai.[11] A disciple of the apostle Paul, however, could not betray any such

10. MT 1 1000CD–1001A, 143.17–144.9, 136–37.

11. Gregory of Nyssa, *The Life of Moses*, trans. Abraham J. Malherbe (New York: Paulist, 1978). Gregory's form of apophatic theology is compared to the Dionysian in the concluding essay of part 2, below.

literary debt. In fact, the Dionysian version is creative and unique but nevertheless tracks one prominent tripartite pattern shared not only with Gregory but also with several other Greek fathers before and after. To begin the ascent with "purification," indeed in a double reference, was conventional. For any reader of Greek, a familiar triad was now expected. Purification is here naturally followed by "contemplation," using the exact word (*theoria*) of the tradition, and then, in the continuation of the text not yet quoted, by "union." Purification, contemplation, and union chart this narrative as an entirely typical Greek progression of spiritual states. In *The Ecclesiastical Hierarchy*, Dionysius uses multiple variations on this triadic terminology, including the pairing of "illumination" with contemplation and "perfection" (or completion) with union, thus appearing to be the apostolic source for a venerable orthodox tradition. Moses, in the Areopagite's narrative, explicitly progresses from purification to contemplation or illumination and then on to perfection or union, as should and do others in his corpus and throughout Greek spiritual writing. The familiar vocabulary of this triadic ascent gives a clear overall itinerary for Moses on Mount Sinai.

But there is another sequence to notice, one with less familiar and very specialized terminology used rarely in this corpus. The "purification" of Moses echoes the liturgical cleansing not only of all believers in Baptism but also of the clerical leader (hierarch) who washes his hands in the eucharistic liturgy.[12] That Moses is then separated from the others has its own liturgical counterpart, as does going beyond the lights and sounds around him. At the summit, Moses is poised to contemplate not the invisible God but "where he dwells," which echoes the Exodus narrative about the thick darkness or cloud. "Contemplation" of the divine milieu is exactly the name

12. For the textual evidence on this overall argument, not only about purification, see the note at MT 1, 137, note 10; and *Commentary*, 190–91.

given to the spiritual interpretation of each liturgical rite in *The Ecclesiastical Hierarchy*. There is word play here amid the complex construction, and perhaps irony, for whatever can be seen by the eye or conceived by the mind (the perceptible and the understandable that the reader has been advised to leave behind) must yield to a dark cloud wherein a presence beyond all sight and thought is encountered somehow. At the top of Mount Sinai, the stage is set for a plunge into what became a famous cloud of unknowing. "But then he [Moses] breaks free of them, away from what sees and is seen, and he plunges into the truly mysterious darkness of unknowing. Here, renouncing all that the mind may conceive, wrapped entirely in the intangible and the invisible, he belongs completely to him who is beyond everything. Here, being neither oneself nor someone else, one is supremely united to the completely unknown [God] by an inactivity of all knowledge, and knows beyond the mind by knowing nothing."[13]

On Sinai's height, Moses is separated from whatever can see or be seen and he enters into the "thick darkness where God was" (Exod. 20:21), also called a "thick cloud" (Exod. 19:16; cf. Ps. 18:11). At this climactic moment, certain individual words carried resonance through the centuries. The biblical "darkness" became famous as *The Cloud of Unknowing* penned by the same medieval Englishman who first translated *The Mystical Theology* as *Denis's Hid Divinity*, as mentioned in part 2 below. That this darkness or cloud is here called "mysterious" is another instance of the Dionysian word "mystical." That this is a darkness "of unknowing" finds an echo a sentence later in the supreme union with the "unknown" (God) as an echo of Paul's invocation of the unknown God in Acts 17.

13. MT 1 1001A, 144.9–15, 137. This translation ("the completely unknown" [God]) corrects the original Paulist printing ("a completely unknowing inactivity") with the help of John of Scythopolis, *Scholia* 421.1, 244.

And yet, words cannot convey this union beyond all sensation and normal knowledge, at least not without multiplying negations.[14] One must renounce knowledge, accept the *in*tangible and *in*visible, and surrender to the "One who is beyond all things," again in the traditional philosophical expression. Even "self" and "other" dissolve in this supreme union, a claim that later "mystics" developed into forms of ecstatic "union without distinction." Being united in this highest way to the "unknown one" of Pauline vintage means a self-transcending discontinuance or inactivity of normal knowledge. What it means to "know beyond the mind by knowing nothing" will take more exposition, below, but Moses amid Sinai's darkness will be its exemplar for centuries.

14. For extensive analysis of Dionysian union, its predecessors and various dimensions, see Ysabel de Andia, *Henosis: L'union à Dieu chez Denys L'Aréopagite* (Leiden: E. J. Brill, 1996).

Chapter Two

Although Moses is left behind as the once and future paragon, our author proceeds in chapter 2 to explicate the same themes of darkness and light, knowing and unknowing. "I pray we could come to this darkness so far above light!"[1] Again, the prefix *hyper-* makes the first of several appearances amid other negations; the "hyperlit darkness" of Sinai will now be explained in more general and less exegetical terms. "If only we lacked sight and knowledge so as to see, so as to know, unseeing and unknowing, that which lies beyond all vision and knowledge."[2] Before following this chapter to the language of denials and thus to Dionysian *un*knowing, we should pause here to note another location in the corpus with exactly the same theme and vocabulary—namely, the enigmatic initial epistles. Letters 1 and 2 trade on darkness and light, knowing and unknowing, using the same vocabulary, negations, and *hyper-* compounds as *The Mystical Theology*. Explicitly advising the reader (this time, the "Gaius" associated with the apostle Paul and 3 John) to receive such negative language "not in terms of deprivation but rather in terms of transcendence," Letter 1 bluntly states that God "transcends mind and being. He is completely unknown and non-existent. He exists

1. MT 2 1025A, 145.1, 138.
2. MT 2 1025A, 145.1–3, 138.

beyond being and he is known beyond the mind."[3] How can this be, asks Letter 2? Because, in short, we are trying to talk about not merely the source of existence or goodness or divinity, which would seem within our grasp, but in fact the one "who transcends every source" and is thus beyond "all grasping."[4] After Letters 3 and 4, which have been endlessly parsed for hints of the author's Christology, Letter 5 resumes the theme of "divine darkness" and "unapproachable light," this time supplying biblical warrant for such superlatives and negations as the Pauline "inscrutable, unsearchable, inexpressible," and so forth.[5]

The epistles continue and cover several crucial issues expounded elsewhere, such as the author's claim to have witnessed an eclipse during the crucifixion (Letter 7) and the extensive concern for hierarchical order in ecclesial affairs (Letter 8).[6] Letter 9 concerns the many and apparently incongruous corporeal characteristics of God in Scripture, if one were to take such external appearances literally. Of course, such symbolic expressions have an inner meaning to be affirmed even as the outer covering is denied in the literal sense. Denials of that specific exegetical sort will make their appearance in *The Mystical Theology* as well, albeit obliquely, but for now chapter 2 continues with a more general observation.

In the rest of chapter 2, the author specifies what it means to see and to know while at the same time being unseeing and unknowing: "For this would be really to see and to know: to praise the Transcendent One in a transcending way, namely, through the denial of all beings. We would be like sculptors who set out to

3. Ep 1 1065A, 157.1–5, 263.
4. Ep 2 1069A, 158.7–11, 263.
5. Citing Exod. 20:21, 1 Tim. 6:16, Rom. 11:33, and 2 Cor. 9:15; Ep 5, 1073A–1076A, 162.3–163.5, 265–66. John's comments on the *Mystical Theology* also refer explicitly to letter 5 regarding "divine darkness." *Scholia* 421.1, 245.
6. See *Commentary*, 18–24, and Hathaway, *Hierarchy and the Definition of Order*.

carve a statue. They remove every obstacle to the pure view of the hidden image, and simply by this act of clearing aside [denial] they show up the beauty which is hidden."[7] Again using synonyms for (sense) perception and understanding as in the opening advice to Timothy—namely, seeing and knowing—the Areopagite here addresses directly what he has suggested in the story of Moses in the darkness. That which lies beyond vision and knowledge can only be seen and known by a special form of *un*seeing and *un*knowing, a specific type of negation or denial. Here the Dionysian vocabulary is convoluted and abstract ("the Transcendent One in a transcending way" is literally "the hyperexistent hyperexistently") and yet also personal and participatory, for the point is "to praise" this transcendent One transcendingly. In this chapter, in the next one on his other works, and throughout his other longest work *The Divine Names*, Dionysius consistently and prominently features the language of praise, literally, "to hymn." In fact, throughout *The Divine Names* the pattern is dominant: we do not neutrally "name" God as Good, One, and so on, but rather we personally "praise" God as Good, One, and the like. To praise the transcendent rightly (in a transcending way) means the "denial" of all beings, a specific form of negation or removal here also translated as "clearing aside." The author's illustration of a sculptor clearing away the obstacles to a hidden beauty is closely connected to the famous essay "On Beauty" by the (Neo-)Platonist Plotinus, where the same illustration is used with the same verbal form for "clearing away."[8] (The early defenders of an apostolic Dionysius had to argue that the third-century Plotinus must have been the borrower here, not the source, but a different textual derivation from the fifth-century Neoplatonist Proclus conclusively proved that our author came after him.[9])

7. MT 2 1025 AB, 145.3–7, 138.
8. *Enneads* I, 6, 9.

In the second half of this chapter (*The Mystical Theology*, chapter 2), we move beyond the darkness of Sinai and the denial or "clearing aside" of all beings to a more complex presentation of "denials" in the plural, not at random but in a specific arrangement:

> Now it seems to me that we should praise the denials quite differently than we do the assertions. When we made assertions we began with the first things, moved down through intermediate terms until we reached the last things. But now as we climb from the last things up to the most primary we deny all things so that we may unhiddenly know that unknowing which itself is hidden from all those possessed of knowing amid all beings, so that we may see above being that darkness concealed from all the light among beings.[10]

Suddenly, assertions and denials, both in the plural, are said to be arranged in specific and separate sequences. A spatial referent recurs, for the assertions seem ordered in a descending sequence from first down to middle to last, while the denials are made in the opposite order, from the last or lowest up to the first. Without other passages, such as especially the next chapter's further exposition of these two interrelated sequences, this spatial imagery as briefly expressed in terms of down and up would be too cryptic. The key to Dionysian talk of "down" and "up" is the late Neoplatonic pattern of "procession and return." In the traditional (manuscript) ordering of his treatises, our author begins his corpus with a programmatic statement along these lines, both revealing and uplifting. "Inspired by the Father, each procession of the Light spreads itself generously toward us, and, in its power to unify, it stirs us by lifting us up. It returns us back to the oneness and deifying simplicity of the Father who gathers us in."[11] Downward procession is thus an enlightening revelation;

9. For Plotinus, see *Scholia*, 118–37; for Proclus and the work of Koch and Stiglmayr in 1895, see *Commentary*, 17.
10. MT 2 1025B, 145.7–14, 138.
11. CH 1 120B, 7.4–7, 145; see note 4.

upward return is a deifying union, as seen throughout the corpus and discussed often.[12] How assertions and especially denials fit into this pattern will become clearer shortly, in the third chapter.

For the moment, the second chapter ends with a restatement of the purpose for such a programmatic denial or removal: it is all in order to know the unknowing that is hidden from ordinary knowing and to see the (again, hyperexistent) darkness concealed from existing light. The chapter here reprises the opening theme of light and darkness but has moved on to specify the sequential arrangements of assertions and denials with no further mention of this visual language. The biblical images of light and darkness and a cloud have served to bring the reader this far, but now the language shifts, starting with self-referential summaries of other works.

One point of terminology: chapter 1 spoke of affirmations and negations, while chapter 2 mentions assertions and denials, with the major allusion to a sculptor's denial (or "removal") along the way. The Dionysian vocabulary always repays close examination; is our author using different terms, specifically, "negations" and "denials," because there is a substantive difference between them or (merely) for some stylistic variety between equivalents? The earliest and now predominant interpretation (and my own) entails a functional equivalence of "negation" (*apophasis*) and "denial" (*aphairesis*), but this might miss an intentional nuance of difference.[13]

12. See, for example, *Biblical and Liturgical Symbols*, 58–65, and *Commentary*, 51–53.
13. The first commentator (John of Scythopolis) took denials and negations as equivalents. See *Scholia* 428A; 425.11, 246. See also PG 4 428C ("Behold an affirmation or assertion . . . behold, a negation or denial") by another later scholiast, not John. For a full-scale rebuttal and alternative, see now Timothy D. Knepper, *Negating Negation: Against the Apophatic Abandonment of the Dionysian Corpus* (Eugene, OR: Cascade Books, 2014), with various scholars mentioned on 36n2. Knepper's argument goes far beyond this terminological distinction, as evident in his chapter titles: "The Divine Names Are Not Names," "Negation Does Not Negate," "Ranks Are Not Bypassed; Rites Are Not Negated," and "The Ineffable God Is Not Ineffable." Knepper takes aim at claims of absolute (even nihilistic) negation in Dionysius as a postmodern malaise, but most careful studies have tried to situate the Areopagite's relative apophatic within his overall interpretive or exegetical method of balancing affirmation and negation.

Chapter Three

By summarizing three previous works, the next chapter seems at first to switch gears from the purposes and patterns of assertions and denials to a literary synopsis of other works, whether extant or perhaps fictitious. But, in fact, the descriptions of prior writings will help explain what Dionysius means by kataphatic or affirmative theology and by descending assertions and ascending denials. Overall, the first half of this chapter gives a detailed description of "The Theological Representations," which may never have been written at all, a terse account of *The Divine Names*, which is the longest treatise and most doctrinally detailed in the corpus, and then an itemized account of "The Symbolic Theology," also nonextant and perhaps never written. As many have pointed out, the two "summaries" along with other cross-references may serve a literary purpose of substituting for the supposedly lost works:

> In my *Theological Representations* I have praised the notions which are appropriate to affirmative theology. I have shown the sense in which the divine and good nature is said to be one and then triune, how Fatherhood and Sonship are predicated of it, the meaning of the theology of the Spirit, how these core lights of goodness grew from the incorporeal and indivisible good, and how in this sprouting they have remained inseparable from their co-eternal foundation in it, in themselves, and in each other. I have spoken of how Jesus, who is above individual being, became a being with a true human nature.

> Other revelations of scripture were also praised in *The Theological Representations*.[1]

The first of the earlier treatises is also presented at the outset of *The Divine Names* as a prior work. In fact, the extant and essential *Divine Names* confirms this trio's sequence, for its very first line hearkens back to "The Theological Representations," and its final words promise a sequel called "The Symbolic Theology."[2]

Taking them one at a time, the contents of "The Theological Representations" (or "Sketches"), as ostensibly summarized here, show a careful sequence of scriptural affirmations: God is one and then triune with explicit naming of Fatherhood and Sonship and the Spirit, and then the (again, hyperexistent) Jesus is incarnated as truly human. The fact that *The Divine Names* also opens with a summary of biblical affirmations in this same sequence (God as one, then three, then incarnate) suggests that these two strategically placed passages did not really summarize a lost treatise but effectively replaced it and thus relieved any need for the author to go into full exposition.[3] "The Theological Representations" is also mentioned along the way in *The Divine Names* to the same effect, namely, that he can be brief about God's unity and trinity here since he says he has elsewhere "provided from scripture a lengthy proof and analysis of the question."[4] Whether "The Theological Representations" was ever written or not, the point here in *The Mystical Theology* is that it initiates a sequence of writings and that it contains within itself

1. MT 3 1032D–1033A, 146.1–9, 138–39.
2. DN 1 585B, 107.3, 49; DN 13, 984A, 231.8, 131.
3. DN 1 589D–592B, 112.7–113.12, 51–52.
4. DN 2 637C, 124.12–15, 60; for further explicit references to *The Theological Representations*, see DN 1 593B, 116.7, 53; DN 2 636C, 122.11, 58; DN 2 640B, 125.13–14, 60; DN 2 645A, 130.15, 63; and DN 11 953B, 221.11, 124. At this summary of Trinitarian theology in *The Mystical Theology*, John's *Scholia* refer to "more recent fathers" who propose "homo-ousian" (*Scholia* 424.3, 246), and they suggest an apostolic preemptive refutation of later heretics like Nestorius (*Scholia* 425.2, 246).

the affirmations, in sequence, of God's unity and then God's triunity. That this movement from simple unity to a certain multiplicity is a descent of assertions will be explained soon, but other works need presentation first.

The Divine Names

The chapter continues with a short summary of a long and famously extant treatise: "In *The Divine Names* I have shown the sense in which God is described as good, existent, life, wisdom, power, and whatever other things pertain to the conceptual names for God."[5] In remarkably few words, this sentence provides an accurate glimpse of the contents of *The Divine Names*, but no hint of its length or complexity. The summary is rendered literally as follows: "In *Concerning the Divine Names*, how [God] is named 'good,' how 'being,' how 'life' and 'wisdom' and 'power' and whatever else is of the conceptual God-naming." That this previous treatise concerns the "conceptual" naming of God is to be taken in tandem with the immediate identification of another treatise on the "perceptible" naming of God, "The Symbolic Theology," as considered shortly. This thematic tandem, already previewed in the opening advice regarding the perceptible and understandable, also structures the last two chapters of *The Mystical Theology*, which describe the way the perceptible and the conceptual are finally to be interpreted by way of negations. As for the specific divine names, those listed here are exactly the subjects of successive chapters in *The Divine Names*, but only after a complex methodological prolegomenon, itself three or four times longer than *The Mystical Theology* as a whole. In fact, the fourth chapter of *The Divine Names* on the "good," so briefly listed here, is itself a thorough philosophical essay also three or four

5. MT 3 1033A, 146.9–11, 139.

times longer than the entire *Mystical Theology*. Such complexity and length mean that we are here barely glimpsing a work of enormous importance and with its own bibliographical domain. Over time, *The Divine Names* has attracted more modern analysis than any other Dionysian treatise, not simply because it is the longest work by far but also because such philosophical contents have stimulated historians of Platonism ever since its relationship to Proclus was established in 1895. The goal here is not to summarize all that philosophical exposition but simply to situate this treatise relative to *The Mystical Theology*.

As mentioned, *The Divine Names* opens with a quick nod back to the prior "Theological Representations" but moves immediately to the prefatory claim that all these names and concepts about God are revealed in Scripture. And yet, the Scripture writers themselves testify to the transcendence of God beyond all names and beyond being itself, as we have seen. "Many scripture writers will tell you that the divinity is not only invisible and incomprehensible, but also 'unsearchable and inscrutable' [Rom. 11:33], since there is not a trace for anyone who would reach through into the hidden depths of this infinity."[6] However, this familiar recognition of divine transcendence does not stand alone but is paired with God's generous communication to and proportionate enlightenment of those who would receive it. Amid his eloquent expositions of this pairing of transcendence and accommodation, Dionysius early in *The Divine Names* indicates how this happens to us, in sequential terms entirely consistent with *The Mystical Theology*: "But as for now, what happens is this. We use whatever appropriate symbols we can for the things of God. With these analogies we are raised upward toward the truth of the mind's vision, a truth which is simple and one. [Then] we leave

6. DN 1 588C, 110.7–10, 50, with further biblical sources and Dionysian cross-references given on 50n6.

behind us all our own notions of the divine. We call a halt to the activities of our minds and, to the extent that is proper, we approach the ray which transcends being."[7] Not only does this last phrase use the same language for a "hyperexistent ray" that concludes *The Mystical Theology*'s opening advice to Timothy, its bipartite structure also and more generally is the same sequence we are encountering in our small treatise: from perceptible symbols up to their conceptual meanings and then beyond any such concepts. Within the enterprise of praising God by name(s), this means, as the opening chapter of *The Divine Names* repeats often, that "as Cause of all and as transcending all, he is rightly nameless and yet has the name of everything that is."[8] After sampling some such (scriptural) names, Dionysius closes his introductory chapter on *The Divine Names* with a warning to Timothy about confidentiality and a prayer that God will allow him to praise aright the numerous names of the unnameable deity.[9]

Yet before proceeding to those names, starting with God as "Good," *The Divine Names* first delves in its second chapter into the complexities of divine unity and distinctions. The main point—that all these divine names apply to the whole divinity, not just to one Trinitarian person—quickly grows into a complex exposition of unities and differentiations best summarized elsewhere.[10] Then, before actually taking up a specific name, the work's third chapter pauses for prayer to the Trinity. Although this is reminiscent of the opening of *The Mystical Theology*, no actual prayer is supplied. Rather, the author reflects on the power of prayer and on the prayerful experiences of his mentor Hierotheus, who here takes his enigmatic place next to the apostle Paul.[11]

7. DN 1 592CD, 115.6–10, 53.
8. DN 1 596C, 119.10–11, 56; see also DN 1 596A, 118.2–3, 54.
9. DN 1 597C, 121.14–18, 58.
10. For the main point, see the opening and closing statements in chapter 2 of *The Divine Names*: DN 2 636C—637A, 122.1–14, 58; DN 2 652A, 137.10–13, 67.

Finally, chapter 4 of *The Divine Names* begins the mentioned sequence of names, starting with God as "Good," but this treatment of one name also stretches on and on through an exposition of beauty and love and especially at some length through a discourse about evil (the absence of good) and its source. Along the way, Dionysius mentions several of his other (lost or fictitious) works, unintentionally reveals his literary debt to Proclus, and in general applies his philosophical system to a wide variety of topics all thoroughly investigated in other studies. His typical treatment of a divine name by way of affirmation and negation can be reduced to simple terms: Scripture calls God "good," yet God is not "good" in our limited sense; this is not to say that God is "bad" but rather that God is "more-than-good" or "hypergood," itself a special form of negation. As listed in *The Mystical Theology*, the name "Being" comes next in chapter 5, then "Life, Wisdom, and Power" in chapters 6 through 8. Other names and concepts are covered along the way, and there are five more chapters still: on "great and small," "Omnipotent and Ancient of Days," "Peace," "Holy of Holies," and especially God as "Perfect and One" in the concluding chapter 13. This representative sampling does not indicate the richness and complexity of these expositions or the importance of this treatise for understanding Dionysian thought as a whole. But the last chapter's topic can introduce a major question and some recent literature. What is the rationale for starting with God as "Good" and ending with God as "One?" Specifically, is there any reason for the order of names and chapters in between the lofty "Good" and the climactic "One"? There have been several partial hypotheses over the years, but recently Christian Schäfer has proposed an overall rationale for the

11. On "Hierotheus," his *Elements of Theology* (also a title by Proclus!), and his spiritual or ritual experience, see *Commentary*, 146–47.

entire sequence, congruent with the author's well-attested use of the Neoplatonic construct of "remaining, procession, and return."[12]

What matters most for our analysis here is not the internal sequence within *The Divine Names* but rather its overall place in a larger sequence of treatises, at least as presented for a reason in *The Mystical Theology*'s third chapter. That sequence continues with mention of another treatise.

The Symbolic Theology

> In my *Symbolic Theology* I have discussed analogies of God drawn from what we perceive. I have spoken of the images we have of him, of the forms, figures, and instruments proper to him, of the places in which he lives and of the ornaments he wears. I have spoken of his anger, grief, and rage, of how he is said to be drunk and hungover, of his oaths and curses, of his sleeping and waking, and indeed of all those images we have of him, images shaped by the workings of the symbolic representations of God.[13]

Like "The Theological Representations," this reference to "The Symbolic Theology" offers a digest of some contents without any such work ever existing, as far as we know. As with the other phantom work, this one is also mentioned early and late in *The Divine Names* and in other places as well. Here and elsewhere, the vocabulary is instructive, for the reference to the "conceptual" divine names in one treatise is followed immediately by a reference to the "perceptible" symbols for God in the next work, extant or not. In general, "symbolic theology" refers to biblical images involving the physical senses, usually the sense of sight. So the examples given here,

12. Christian Schäfer, *The Philosophy of Dionysius the Areopagite: An Introduction to the Structure and the Content of the Treatise On the Divine Names* (Leiden: Brill, 2006). More recently still, Stephen Gersh has turned his philosophical analysis toward the same question: "Dionysius' *On Divine Names* Revisited: A Structural Analysis," *Dionysius* 28 (2010): 77–96.

13. MT 3 1033AB, 146.11–147.3, 139.

and more fully elsewhere, are of the scriptural depictions of God's appearance, such as God's "back" as seen by Moses (Exod. 33:23), obviously symbolic. Such images can go beyond bodily features to unbecoming activities such as God's anger or rage, drinking to excess, cursing or sleeping, all biblical allusions mentioned here but not interpreted. For fuller lists and our author's creative exegesis, we need to turn to other places where "The Symbolic Theology" is discussed in more detail. The opening of *The Divine Names* identifies its own subject as the conceptual names for God rather than the perceptible features mentioned in Scripture: "eyes, ears, hair, face, and hands, back, wings, and arms, a posterior and feet," with "crowns, chairs, cups and mixing bowls" placed around. Such items, he says, will be interpreted when he moves on to "The Symbolic Theology."[14] Other brief references to this treatise within *The Divine Names* serve the same function of postponing any exegetical content.[15] Yet, there is also one mention of "The Symbolic Theology" that is accompanied by considerable exegesis of what such perceptible biblical symbols really mean, including some of those mentioned in this part of *The Mystical Theology*. The long Letter 9 explicitly invokes "The Symbolic Theology" at its outset and again at its conclusion, and in between it actually supplies interpretations of many such perceptible symbols, including the "anger, grief, and rage," the drinking and hangover, and the "oaths and curses," along with dozens of other such symbols. Not all of the items listed in Letter 9 are then interpreted later in the epistle, but the divine inebriation and sleep are given careful attention as God's form of ecstatic excess and divine transcendence.[16] More on how to interpret such apparent

14. DN 1 597B, 120.15—121.3, 57.
15. DN 4 700D, 149.9, 75 (where a verb was supplied, wrongly, in the past tense); DN 9 913B, 211.7–9, 117; DN 13 984A, 231.7–8, 131 (the very last words of *The Divine Names*). See also the quick reference to the four elements, including wind, in CH 15 336A, 56.1–2, 187.
16. Ep 9 1105B, 195.8–196.1, 282. Ep 9 1112B–1113B, 204.8–206.12, 287–88.

incongruities is yet to come, including the exegetical method presented at the outset of *The Celestial Hierarchy*.

As mentioned, the start of the third chapter of *The Mystical Theology* seems at first to be simply this literary synopsis of previous works. But the way they are summarized leads the reader back to the second chapter's terse topic of descending assertions and ascending denials. The very contents of these three treatises have already suggested a thematic progression, also sketched at the beginning of *The Divine Names*: from God's unity and trinity ("The Theological Representations") to the various conceptual names for God (*The Divine Names*) and finally to the many symbolic representations ("The Symbolic Theology"). This material sequence from unity and simplicity to plurality and multiplicity now turns out to carry a formal sequence regarding the apparent relative length of these three works. "And I feel sure that you have noticed how these latter come much more abundantly than what went before, since *The Theological Representations* and a discussion of the names appropriate to God are inevitably briefer than what can be said in *The Symbolic Theology*."[17]

Of course, only one of these works can be measured for length, but the claim for a progression of increasing size provides the transition from literary description back to the enigmatic issue of descending assertions and ascending denials. That "The Theological Representations" should be briefer than *The Divine Names* is not hard to imagine, since its subject matter is a large but single package of Trinitarian material along with the incarnation. Even a full treatment thereof could easily be briefer than the lengthy *Divine Names*. There is also a thematic logic in movement from divine unity to trinity to the multiple names for God in Scripture. Then, although the next logical progression still holds (from the moderate assortment

17. MT 3 1033B, 147.4–7, 139.

of conceptual divine names to the profuse abundance of perceptible symbols for God), the sheer length of *The Divine Names* would require "The Symbolic Theology" to be enormous. Yet, relative size does become important, not so much for the treatises just surveyed but for what is to come. The thematic flow just sketched also hints at the "downward" movement in question, more explicitly in the first chapter of *The Divine Names* as cited but also in the relative place of unity above trinity and the conceptual above the perceptible.

At this point, from the middle of *The Mystical Theology*'s middle chapter, the text presents such a compressed account of the author's overall theological method that we need to notice every detail. Repeated paraphrases may be needed in the attempt to convey some of the complexities. The very next sentence invokes the spatial metaphor as linked to verbal expression, not regarding a downward expansion but rather an upward contraction. "The fact is that the more we take flight upward, the more our words are confined to the ideas we are capable of forming; so that now as we plunge into that darkness which is beyond intellect, we shall find ourselves not simply running short of words but actually speechless and unknowing."[18] Suddenly, Moses' ascent and plunge into a darkness of unknowing beyond the mind has become our itinerary too, in identical terminology. A literary counterpart is also added, for this ascent is an upward constriction of words and concepts all the way up to silence and unknowing.

Here the author himself seems to provide a paraphrase of his previous sentences about a downward expansion of assertions and an upward contraction of denials. "In the earlier (books) my argument traveled downward from the most exalted to the humblest categories, taking in on this downward path an ever-increasing number of

18. MT 3 1033B, 147.7–10, 139. Perhaps, more accurately, "confined by our glimpses of the conceptual things."

ideas which multiplied with every stage of the descent."[19] Using a then/now construction, Dionysius has first repeated what he just summarized about his prior works, specifying again that the downward path from exalted ideas (divine unity and trinity) to humblest categories (divine drunkenness and sleep) entails an "ever-increasing" multiplication of content and thus longer works. With verbs in the past tense, that was "then."

"Now" comes the reverse sequence, the upward contraction of speech and concepts so characteristic of Dionysian mystical theology. "But my argument now rises from what is below up to the transcendent, and the more it climbs, the more language falters, and when it has passed up and beyond the ascent, it will turn silent completely, since it will finally be at one with him who is indescribable."[20] Here the author reprises his theme about the ascending reduction of language until the silent union with the indescribable one. As with the example of Moses, there is finally, after every ascent, a unification with the ineffable in silence. A final union with the "unknown" (God) is where the Areopagite's spiritual itinerary ultimately culminates, but it is hard to describe or understand, almost by definition, and harder still to attain. "Now you may wonder why . . ." (literally, "why, you say, do we . . ."), continues the text, and the reader may well wonder why on several levels.

"Now You May Wonder Why . . ."

For the moment, the author specifies another complex dimension within the pattern of descending assertions and ascending denials. "Now you may wonder why it is that, after starting out from the highest category when our method involved assertions, we begin

19. MT 3 1033C, 147.10–12, 139.
20. MT 3 1033C, 147.12–14, 139.

now from the lowest category when it involves a denial."[21] As in chapter 2, the specific starting point for the descending assertions is the "highest" or "first," while for the ascending (divine) denials we start with the "lowest" or "last" things. But why? (And, might some examples help?) For the difficult and compressed wording in the rest of this chapter, we start with a literal translation and then explicate it with paraphrases. "Because, in asserting what is beyond every assertion it is necessary to assert the underlying [hypothetical] affirmation from what is more closely related to it. But in denying what is beyond every denial it is necessary to deny from what are more separated from it."[22] Such cryptic wording was necessarily but approximately paraphrased in print as follows: "The reason is this. When we assert what is beyond every assertion, we must then proceed from what is most akin to it, and as we do so we make the affirmation on which everything else depends. But when we deny that which is beyond every denial, we have to start by denying those qualities which differ most from the goal we hope to attain."[23] This expanded wording is still not enough to explain the author's meaning, but coming into view is the notion that some affirmations about God seem closer to the truth than others, and some denials about God seem more obviously true than others. Perhaps some biblical examples? "Is [God] not more life and goodness than air or stone? And more not drunk and not raving than not spoken or thought?"[24] Quickly mentioned here, "air" (the still small breeze of 1 Kgs. 19:12) and "stone" (Ps. 118:22) are exegeted elsewhere, as already noted and covered more fully shortly. Here too the extreme brevity requires a more expansive paraphrase or two: "Is it not closer to reality to say that God is life and goodness rather than that he is air

21. MT 3 1033C, 147.15–16, 139.
22. MT 3 1033C, 147.16–19.
23. MT 3 1033C, 147.16–19, 139–40.
24. MT 3 1033CD, 147.19–21.

or stone? Is it not more accurate to deny that drunkenness and rage can be attributed to him than to deny that we can apply to him the terms of speech and thought? (Or, is it not more incorrect to say that God gets drunk or raves than that he is expressed or conceived?)"[25]

We cannot understand this way of arranging assertions and denials until we realize that they are not uniform categories but rather a sliding scale of congruity and incongruity. Although these categories (congruity and incongruity, and thus assertions and denials) are actually inseparable and indeed simultaneous,[26] they can be separated into a specific sequence for pedagogical reasons. Yes, all assertions about God fall short of capturing the transcendent One exactly, as Dionysius says often. But not all assertions are completely inappropriate; some come close, while others seem hopelessly incongruent. They can be arranged in a descending order of decreasing congruity (or increasing incongruity). Affirmative theology can start with the highest or most fitting assertions (God's unity and trinity in "The Theological Representations"), move "down" a little to the other concepts about God (*The Divine Names*), and then descend further to the numerous physical symbols for the divine ("The Symbolic Theology"). Similarly, negations about God may all be equally true, grammatically speaking, for God is beyond and thus *not* anything our finite language might attempt. But such denials are not all the same. They too can be arranged in a pedagogical sequence, starting with denials of the most obviously incongruous or absurd characteristics. To deny such perceptible symbols for God as air or stone, or drunkenness or rage, means to *understand* the biblical language as symbolic, as not true on the one (literal) level but rather pointing to a spiritual truth of a higher order. In that sense, negations of the perceptible are part of biblical

25. MT 3 1033CD, 147.19–21, 140 with note 17.
26. See *Commentary*, 203–4.

interpretation yielding conceptual truths. Yet those truths or concepts must also be negated or left behind in Dionysian recognition that God transcends even our highest concepts or loftiest names. The earlier advice to Timothy about leaving behind the perceptible and the conceptual has already previewed a large share of this Dionysian spiritual method, as also glimpsed in the compressed wording of the final two chapters.

Chapter Four

Although the chapter titles may not be original with our author, they are often indicative of the contents, as in the (paraphrased) translations supplied for the last two chapters of *The Mystical Theology*. Chapter 4 is titled "That the Supreme Cause of Every Perceptible Thing Is Not Itself Perceptible." Chapter 5 is titled "That the Supreme Cause of Every Conceptual Thing Is Not Itself Conceptual."[1] Here the pairing of the perceptible and conceptual invokes the supreme cause of both, and it turns negative. Yet because denials operate differently in the two domains, we need a careful transition from the biblical examples at the end of chapter 3 to these two paragraphs crammed with negations. Fortunately, another Dionysian work addresses apophatic theology quite directly, specifically examining the role of negations in biblical interpretation and thus the concept of relative congruity and incongruity. *The Celestial Hierarchy*, chapter 2, can elucidate the apophatic method at work in *The Mystical Theology*, especially regarding the transition from the biblical allusions at the end of its third chapter to the negations of the perceptible in chapter 4.

1. MT 4 1040D and MT 5 1045D, 148.1 and 149.1, citing variant readings from later manuscripts, 140 and 141.

Worthy of the extended commentary it has historically received in its own right, *The Celestial Hierarchy* is not simply about the angels, at least not at first.[2] The opening three chapters are about God and revelation in general, including the role of negations in the theological interpretation of Scripture. Since the biblical texts reveal the celestial beings by way of material and even bestial appearances, some careful exegesis is needed in order to receive the intended meaning.[3] "The Word of God makes use of poetic imagery when discussing these formless intelligences but, as I have already said, it does so not for the sake of art, but as a concession to the nature of our own mind. It uses scriptural passages in an uplifting way, provided for us from the first, to uplift our mind in a manner suitable to our nature."[4] This last sentence alone has four (Greek) indicators of the "upward" or "anagogical" thrust of this interpretive movement, as discussed at some length elsewhere.[5] The gist of this chapter for understanding *The Mystical Theology* with its own ascent language is in the complex notion of dissimilar similarities.[6] God, as we have seen, may be named as Word or Being, yet these apparently fitting affirmations finally fall short of the transcendent unknown One. Negations, however, such as "*in*visible" or "*in*finite," are another matter. The pivotal sentence is translated literally as follows: "If, therefore, negations regarding the divine things are true on the one hand and (if) on the other hand affirmations are unbefitting to the hiddenness of the ineffable, then a manifestation through dissimilar shapings is rather more appropriate to the invisible."[7] A

2. For Eriugena, see *Eriugena's Commentary*; for Hugh of St. Victor, see *Hugh of St. Victor*, 167–76, and the essay on both of them in part 2, below.
3. CH 2 137A, 10.1–8, 147–48.
4. CH 2 137B, 10.9–12, 148.
5. *Biblical and Liturgical Symbols*, ch. 7, "The Anagogical Movement," 99–116.
6. For fuller commentary on the whole of *The Celestial Hierarchy*, ch. 2, see *Biblical and Liturgical Symbols*, ch. 6, "Biblical Absurdities," 84–96, and *Commentary*, 53–57.
7. CH 2 141A, 12.20–13.3.

looser paraphrase would render the sentence thus: "Since the way of negation appears to be more suitable to the realm of the divine and since positive affirmations are always unfitting to the hiddenness of the inexpressible, a manifestation through dissimilar shapes is more correctly to be applied to the invisible."[8]

In giving some examples, this chapter of *The Celestial Hierarchy* confirms not only that this interpretive insight applies to passages about God as well as the angels, but also that such "dissimilar similarities"[9] can be understood on a continuum from the lofty and apparently similar symbols for God (such as sun or light) down through intermediate images (such as fire or water), even sinking to the lowly and apparently incongruous dissimilarities (such as a stone or an animal, even a worm).[10] That these images are on a continuum allows or even intends the reverse and uplifting direction of first admitting that God is not really an animal, or light, or even (as we climb higher) Word or Being, insofar as all perceptions and concepts fail.[11] This is the same ascent of sequential denials that we have glimpsed in *The Mystical Theology*. Denying the lower realm first and then the higher applies both to the lower and higher perceptible (biblical) symbols, as we see here in the second chapter of *The Celestial Hierarchy*, and also to the sequence of using negations first within that lower realm of sense perception as a whole (*The Mystical Theology*, chapter 4) and then "as we climb higher" within the more elevated realm of the conceptual (*The Mystical Theology*, chapter 5).[12] And yet the role of negations varies significantly in the two realms and thus the two chapters, which we are now ready to quote.

8. CH 2 141A, 12. 20–13.3, 150.
9. CH 2 137D, 11.6–7, 148; 141C, 14.1–2, 151; 144A, 14.11, 151.
10. CH 2 144CD, 15.8–21, 152.
11. CH 2 145B, 16.7–13, 153.
12. MT 5 1045D, 149.1, 141.

That the supreme Cause of every perceptible thing is not itself perceptible

"So this is what we say. The Cause of all is above all and is not inexistent, lifeless, speechless, mindless."[13] First to be noted is that this grammatical subject, the "Cause of all," applies to the rest of chapters 4 and 5 without explicitly reappearing until the end of chapter 5. In between, a pronoun ("it") must be supplied again and again.[14] Back in chapter 1, the "cause of all" was associated especially with affirmations derived from its effects, but here it is linked to an exhaustive litany of negations. This apophatic sequence is not random, however, but reflects the same sequence of ascending (and constricting) denials already mentioned.

Without tending to this question of sequence, chapter 4 of *The Mystical Theology* might seem like an arbitrary list of negations. Indeed, some of them do seem random, but not all. As a whole, the chapter would seem to be about the realm of the perceptible, as the (editorial) chapter title indicates. Although the text ends that way, it begins with something else, as just quoted and here supplied more literally: "We say, therefore, that the cause of all, being also beyond all, is neither inexistent nor unliving, neither un-word nor un-mind."[15] Unlike the rest of the chapter, existence and life with word and mind are not the perceptible categories to receive negation but rather conceptual terms. The double negatives here have a special function at the outset of a series of (ascending) denials. From the second chapter of *The Celestial Hierarchy* we know that the starting point for negative theology is a matter of strategic pedagogy: begin where the beginners can begin and then escort them along to a

13. MT 4 1040D, 148.1–2, 140.
14. In John's *Scholia*, the later subject supplied is the "Trinity," which seems to exempt that language from the apophatic principle. *Scholia*, 429.3, 248; see also 70.
15. MT 4 1040D, 148.1–2.

higher, intermediate level and then higher still to the advanced forms of negations. For the novice, the thought that God does not exist, or is lifeless or mindless, is objectionable and can be denied immediately. Ironically, the more advanced Dionysian disciple must in fact say (just a page later!) that God does *not* have existence or mind as we know it. But here at the start of the sequence, the novice can make these elementary denials.[16] After them come the negations of the perceptible realm regarding the cause of all, some of them seemingly haphazard but centering and ending with the terminology of sense perception.

> It [the Cause of all] is not a material body, and hence has neither shape nor form, quality, quantity, or weight. It is not in any place and can neither be seen nor be touched. It is neither perceived nor is it perceptible. It suffers neither disorder nor disturbance and is overwhelmed by no earthly passion. It is not powerless and subject to the disturbances caused by sense perception. It endures no deprivation of light. It passes through no change, decay, division, loss, no ebb and flow, nothing of which the senses may be aware. None of all of this can either be identified with it nor attributed to it.[17]

The last printed sentence could better convey the chapter's culmination of no less than five explicit references to the "perceptible" if it were rendered more literally: the cause of all "neither is nor has anything else of the perceptible."[18] The whole point here is that the transcendent God is "neither perceived nor perceptible,"[19] as aptly summarized in the chapter title even if not original to the author: "That the supreme Cause of every perceptible thing is not itself perceptible." Illustrating this central theme are various aspects of the world of sense perception: shape, weight, place, disorder, change,

16. An early scholiast, not John, says that the author here needs to reassure his readers that the negations yet to come do not mean that God does not even exist. PG 4 428D.
17. MT 4 1040D, 148.2–8, 141.
18. MT 4 1040D, 148.8.
19. MT 4 1040D, 148.4f–5, 141.

decay. Being the cause of all this, and above it all, God is recognized as being beyond such things insofar as we deny or negate them as falling short of the transcendent. In that way, we ascend beyond sense perception toward God. The Sinai story narrated this process in one vivid way; here a staccato list of negatives abruptly entails the same ascent in a more abstract or theoretical way.

The Celestial and Ecclesiastical Hierarchies

By itself, this chapter on negating the realm(s) of sense perception would be too abrupt and abstract, but this form of the apophatic or negative methodology is fully presented elsewhere, especially in *The Celestial Hierarchy*, chapter 2, described earlier. From their titles, it might seem unlikely that *The Celestial Hierarchy* and *The Ecclesiastical Hierarchy* (both full-scale works) have a close relationship to the fourth chapter of *The Mystical Theology*, but the role of negative theology within the interpretation of perceptible symbols links these components of the Dionysian corpus.[20] As mentioned, *The Celestial Hierarchy* begins by specifying the role of negations in (sequentially) understanding the various biblical symbols for God and the angels, starting with those incongruities that are easiest to deny. That God is not a worm is easy enough to say, but how should we read Ps. 22:6 or other biblical passages that use the sun or light to characterize the divine, not to mention all the visible (perceptible) attributes given to the angels? As a whole, *The Celestial Hierarchy* covers all these interpretive questions and cannot really be reduced to a few paragraphs.[21] That it interprets perceptible symbols by way of negations is immediately apparent in chapters 1 and 2, with much

20. Against J. Vanneste, *Le Mystére de Dieu* (Paris: De Brouwer, 1959), see my arguments of terminological overlap between the "mystical" and the liturgical in *Biblical and Liturgical Symbols*, 132–42.

21. See *Commentary*, 47–73.

more about the celestial beings added along the way. This interpretive process is explicitly uplifting or anagogical; indeed, the interpretations are called "upliftings." God has used these perceptible forms so that "we might be uplifted from these venerable images to interpretations [upliftings] and assimilations."[22] A biblical symbol for God is almost by definition "both similar and dissimilar to God," as Dionysius says elsewhere, using the same terminology as the "dissimilar similarities" of *The Celestial Hierarchy*, chapter 2.[23] Insofar as a biblical symbol trades on sense perception such as earthly light, it is a dissimilarity to be denied, for God is not earthly. But insofar as this symbolic language is rightly interpreted for its higher meaning, namely, that God is the source of our spiritual enlightenment, then there is here a similarity to be affirmed. Such is the normal process of interpreting perceptible symbols, an uplifting that contains a negation insofar as one leaves behind the lower perceptible level and ascends to the higher conceptual truth. *The Celestial Hierarchy* itself goes on for many chapters to summarize the scriptural revelations about the angelic beings: the notion of a hierarchy, the common name "angel," their specific triadic ranks (seraphim, cherubim, thrones; dominions, powers, authorities; principalities, archangels, angels), and some exegetical puzzles. In its last chapter, it returns to the details of their perceptible appearances, such as human body parts, clothing or weapons, and even animal features. All of this biblical material is to be interpreted with a dose of negation, for the superficial appearances are denied on the way up to higher truths. The "perceptible" is negated, as in the fourth chapter of *The Mystical Theology*, not in the sense of rejecting it flatly but rather in the sense

22. CH 1 121C, 8.17–19, 146; see also CH 15 337D, 58.6, 190, for another use of "anagogy" to mean interpretive uplifting.
23. DN 9 916A, 212.12–13, 118.

of using it rightly in this fruitful interpretive process of rising above the senses to the conceptual level, as in the next chapter.

But there is another hierarchical treatise to consider (*The Ecclesiastical Hierarchy*) and another form of revealed perceptible symbols (the liturgical rites). That these two hierarchical treatises are paired in this order is clear not only from their titles and order in the manuscript tradition, but also from the author's own comments. Early in *The Ecclesiastical Hierarchy*, Dionysius says he has already written about "the hierarchy of angels, archangels," and the like (then naming all nine celestial ranks),[24] and he is presenting our human hierarchy, "pluralized in a great variety of perceptible symbols lifting us upward hierarchically until we are brought as far as we can into the unity of divinization."[25] The angelic minds covered in the prior treatise know God in their own way, but our human situation entails the interpretation of the perceptible in order to rise up to contemplate the divine. Dionysius here introduces liturgical interpretation in terms consonant with *The Mystical Theology*'s Mount Sinai and ascent beyond the perceptible: "It is by way of the perceptible images that we are uplifted as far as we can be to the contemplation of what is divine."[26] This major work then presents and interprets the three sacraments (Baptism, the Eucharist, and myron consecration), the threefold clergy (hierarchs, priests, and deacons), the lay orders (especially monks), and finally funerals. In each chapter, the format is the same: a ritual is described, specifically for the activities or perceptible movements that take place, and then it is interpreted for its higher conceptual meanings. In Baptism, for example, the clergy assist the candidate's undressing and turning from west to east as visible (perceptible) actions that have a conceptual meaning or

24. EH 1 372C, 64.15–23, 196.
25. EH 1 373A, 65. 10–13, 197.
26. EH 1 373B, 65.14–15, 197.

"contemplation"; namely, "having abandoned evil he may in perfect purity endure and look up to the divine Light."[27] Such glimpses into the way Dionysius wished to present the rites of a community, including ordination and monastic tonsure, are extremely interesting in their own right and more fully presented elsewhere.[28] The point here is that such liturgical interpretation is the same uplifting toward the divine by way of the perceptible that we have noted exegetically in *The Celestial Hierarchy* and suggestively in *The Mystical Theology*. Speaking of the myron consecration rite, he says, "After we have examined in detail the sacred imagery its parts present, we shall thus be uplifted in hierarchical contemplations through its parts to the One."[29] Thus, in broad strokes, when *The Mystical Theology* alludes to ascending through and beyond "the perceptible," it encompasses both the biblical perceptible images for the angels in *The Celestial Hierarchy* and also the liturgical perceptible images in *The Ecclesiastical Hierarchy*, and yet with a significant difference.

The biblical exegesis presented in *The Celestial Hierarchy* explicitly incorporated negation into the interpretation of dissimilar similarities, in perfect harmony with the negation of the perceptible in *The Mystical Theology*, chapter 4. But the liturgical interpretation in *The Ecclesiastical Hierarchy* breathes not a word of negation or apophatic methodology. Such ritual symbols are never called incongruous or dissimilar, but rather "precise images" that "appropriately" convey the sacred.[30] On the face of it, *The Ecclesiastical Hierarchy* thus seems far removed from the negations

27. EH 2 401B, 76.16–17, 206. This portion of the section explicitly called "contemplation" interprets ritual actions described earlier in EH 2 396B, 72.1–7, 202–3.
28. See *Commentary*, part 3, 91–117, and Pseudo-Dionysius, *Dionysius the Areopagite: The Ecclesiastical Hierarchy*, ed. Thomas L. Campbell (Washington, DC: University Press of America, 1981).
29. EH 4 472D, 95.5–7, 224. For the parallel wording in biblical interpretation, see CH 4 177C, 20.4–7, 156.
30. EH 2 401C and 404B, 77.8 and 24–25, 207.

of the perceptible in the fourth chapter of *The Mystical Theology*. My argument for holding them together can be only mentioned here, finding fuller expression elsewhere, for it is not essential to the flow of the brief treatise before us. In Dionysian hermeneutics, all perceptible symbols are both similar and dissimilar to the higher conceptual truth conveyed, but one should start with the obvious dissimilarities in order to get beyond literal appearances. Once this form of negation is incorporated into the interpretative method, it is naturally applied to all perceptible symbols in order to go beyond even the congruous language to the higher truth.[31] Thus, even the lofty biblical similarities and the fitting liturgical images are interpreted with an implicit dose of negation in that the literal or physical sense of the perceptible object or action is left behind in the ascent to its higher conceptual meaning. Supporting this argument, although obliquely, is the further difference between the two hierarchical treatises here glimpsed, namely, that the former concerned the spatial sense perception of objects (bodies, robes, weapons) attributed to the angels, while the latter concerned the temporal sense perception of movements or activities (disrobing, turning east, and so forth) in the rites. In one way, the transition from objects and spatial perception to actions and temporal perception is itself a progression from the less congruous to the more fitting, but both realms are interpreted with intertwined negation and affirmation.[32] In any case, we need to return to the transition from chapter 4 to chapter 5 of *The Mystical Theology*.

31. See CH 15 337C, 58.4–6, 189.
32. The fuller argument for this reading of *The Ecclesiastical Hierarchy* is in *Commentary*, 206–10.

Chapter Five

That the Supreme Cause of Every Conceptual Thing is Not Itself Conceptual

In a single opening phrase, chapter 5 confirms an important structural sequence in the Dionysian mystical theology. "Again, as we climb higher, we say this."[1] The movement from the perceptible (chapter 4) to the conceptual (chapter 5) was signaled early on in the opening advice to Timothy. Indeed, the movement advised there was the ascent invoked here and so often; striving upward, "leave behind you everything perceived and understood, everything perceptible and understandable."[2] The fifth chapter of *The Mystical Theology* makes this sequential ascent explicit: "Again, as we climb higher we say this." The ensuing chain of negations parallels those in chapter 4 in the same way that the traditional title for chapter 5 parallels that of chapter 4, but the content in chapter 5 has shifted from sense perception to the intellectual realm of concepts. We have seen that in the realm of the perceptible symbols of the Bible (or the liturgy), negations function alongside affirmations in the interpretation of the symbol to yield its meaning: "light" can mean not the physical phenomenon but spiritual enlightenment. In that realm, negations

1. MT 5 1045D, 149.1, 141.
2. MT 1 997B, 142.5–9, 135.

help lift us up from the physical senses to the concepts that are symbolically conveyed. Yet now, in this chapter, such concepts are themselves negated, and rigorously so: "It is not soul or mind, nor does it possess imagination, conviction, speech, or understanding. Nor is it speech per se, understanding per se. It cannot be spoken of and it cannot be grasped by understanding."[3] By itself, such a litany of negations would seem to reject Christian content, with more negations and more explicit negations yet to come. This denial of "speech," for example, seems to be a rejection of the Johannine language of "logos." Yet, *The Mystical Theology* does not stand by itself but follows *The Divine Names*; such an apparent rejection of names like "logos" is not meant to be taken by itself but rather in light of the exposition of such names in the prior treatise. Negations, explained *The Divine Names* early and often, indicate biblically not that God lacks a quality but that God transcends that quality as its source and cause.[4] In the chapter on "logos" and wisdom and mind, the very concepts receiving abrupt negation here, *The Divine Names* explains: "But, as I have often said previously, we must interpret the things of God in a way that befits God, and when we talk of God as being without mind and without perception, this is to be taken in the sense of what he has in superabundance and not as a defect. Hence we attribute absence of reason [literally, "un-logos"] to him because he is above reason/logos."[5] That this chapter of *The Mystical Theology* must be read in light of *The Divine Names* is obvious not only from its earlier reference back to the prior treatise but also from the way this final dose of negations continues: "It is not number or order, greatness or smallness, equality or inequality,

3. MT 5 1045D, 149.1–3, 141.
4. John of Scythopolis often referred readers of his scholia back to *The Divine Names* and to his comments there regarding denials and unknowing: *Scholia* 417.2, p. 243; 421.1, p. 244; 424.1, p. 245; 425.11, p. 247.
5. DN 7 869A, 196.8–10, 107.

similarity or dissimilarity. It is not immovable, moving, or at rest."[6] These are exactly the terms interpreted in *The Divine Names*, chapter 9: "Greatness and smallness, sameness and difference, similarity and dissimilarity, rest and motion—these all are titles applied to the Cause of everything. They are divinely named images and we should now contemplate them as far as they are revealed to us."[7] Such contemplation there involved a careful juxtaposition of affirmation and negation, "for the very same things are both similar and dissimilar to God."[8] But here in *The Mystical Theology* the point is the negation, the dissimilarity because, as *The Divine Names* has already made explicit, such names or concepts "are dissimilar to him [God] in that as effects they fall so very far short of their Cause and are infinitely and incomparably subordinate to him."[9]

And so it goes for yet more of the negations in the fifth chapter of *The Mystical Theology*. The list continues with "power" and "life," exactly the topics of *The Divine Names*, chapters 8 and 6, respectively: "It has no power, it is not power, nor is it light. It does not live nor is it life. It is not a substance [being], nor is it eternity or time."[10] That God is not power or life because God is "more-than-power" (hyperpower) or beyond life can be taken in stride by someone who has patiently read *The Divine Names*. But the negations (that God is not a being!?) are more and more challenging, coming fast and relentless at the apparent center of Christian content: "It cannot be grasped by the understanding since it is neither knowledge nor truth. It is not kingship. It is not wisdom. It is neither one nor oneness, divinity nor goodness. Nor is it a spirit, in the sense in which we understand that term. It is not sonship or fatherhood

6. MT 5 1045D, 149.3–5, 141.
7. DN 9 909B, 207.6–9, 115.
8. DN 9 916A, 212.12–13, 118.
9. DN 9 916A, 212.13–15, 118.
10. MT 5 1048A, 149.5–7, 141.

and it is nothing known to us or to any other being."[11] Dionysian apophatic theology is approaching its apex. That God is "neither one nor oneness, divinity nor goodness" may seem to reverse the loftiest assertions of *The Divine Names*, except that the earlier treatise had itself explained how such names were to be both asserted and also denied. Even the triune and biblical language of "The Theological Representations" (Father, Son, Spirit) is here abruptly negated, at least "in the sense in which we understand."[12] Here, too, *The Divine Names* had included that bold move in its concluding explanation of "one" and three: "That the transcendent Godhead is one and triune must not be understood in any of our own typical senses. . . . But no unity or trinity, no number or oneness, no fruitfulness, indeed, nothing that is or is known can proclaim that hiddenness beyond every mind and reason of the transcendent Godhead which transcends every being. There is no name for it nor expression [logos]."[13] Echoing this last phrasing ("neither name nor logos"), the principle of negation is pressed even further as *The Mystical Theology* approaches its conclusion: "It falls neither within the predicate of nonbeing nor of being. Existing beings do not know it as it actually is and it does not know them as they are. There is no speaking [logos] of it, nor name nor knowledge of it. Darkness and light, error and truth, it is none of these."[14] This passage begins simply enough; the Cause of all is "not something among nonbeings nor something among beings." Then, a predictable claim—that beings do not know it as it transcendently is—becomes more challenging when reversed: it does not know them as they are. On the face of it, this would seem to place finite limits on the divine knowledge, but perhaps the first

11. MT 5 1048A, 149.7–150.1, 141.

12. An early commentator, not John, wanted this qualification of the apophatic to apply to all of these negations. PG 4 429B.

13. DN 13 980D–981A, 229.6–8 and 10–14, 129.

14. MT 5 1048A, 150.2–5, 141.

Dionysian commentator (John of Scythopolis) is right that the intent is the opposite: God does not know finite beings in their finite way, that is, by the sense perception befitting perceptible objects, since God's knowledge transcends such lower forms of knowing.[15] Even with this plausible explanation, the wording here contributes to the effect that the chapter is building to an apophatic flourish, that God is so far beyond our realm that "there is no speaking of it, nor name nor knowledge of it." After this global negative, our author steps back from making such specific denials to conclude with his final methodological comment *about* assertions and denials. To translate the ending of *The Mystical Theology* rather literally: "Overall, there is neither assertion nor denial of it, but of things after it; in making assertions and denials we are neither asserting nor denying it, for beyond every assertion is the perfect and unique cause of all things and beyond every denial [is] the preeminence of what is simply freed from all things and beyond everything."[16] As assertions and denials were paired back in chapter 2 with reference to gradual descent and ascent, here at the end of the treatise they are paired again as both falling short. Denials of the perceptible served the interpretation of symbolic language in order to assert the intended concepts, but, climbing higher, any such concepts were then also denied as less than the final goal. *The Mystical Theology* ends with no restatement of that goal, only this recognition that assertions and denials are not enough. The printed, more paraphrased version of that finale is as follows: "It is beyond assertion and denial. We make assertions and denials of what is next to it, but never of it, for it is both beyond every assertion,

15. Such at least is the friendly interpretation given at some length by John in *Scholia* 429.3, 247–48. Another comment shows explicit concern for the sensitive reader: "Do not let this chapter disturb you and do not think that this divine man is blaspheming. For his purpose is to show that God is not a being among beings, but is beyond beings. For if [God] himself has brought forth all beings in creation, how can he be found to be one being among other beings." PG 4 429C.

16. MT 5 1048B, 150.5–9.

being the perfect and unique cause of all things, and, by virtue of its preeminently simple and absolute nature, free of every limitation, beyond every limitation, it is also beyond every denial."[17] Here the treatise ends. Indeed, if assertions and denials alike are no longer any use, there is no more to say. The verbal and mental process, now stilled, gives way to silence.[18] The treatise ends abruptly: it (the unknown Cause of all) is beyond everything, beyond even every denial. Yet this silence is not empty.

The abrupt end of *The Mystical Theology* can be read in the light of the finale of *The Divine Names*. As here noted often enough, the apophatic method of assertions and simultaneous denials was also at work in that earlier and longer treatise. Indeed, the brevity of *The Mystical Theology* is linked, explicitly and implicitly, to the fuller accounts of negative theology in the prior work. As quoted above, *The Divine Names* concluded by recognizing that even the loftiest names of "Good" and "One" and "Three" fail to capture the transcendent Godhead. The Scripture writers themselves thus use negations and use them with a definite purpose or goal.

> That is why their preference is for the way up through negations, since this stands the soul outside everything which is correlative with its own finite nature. Such a way guides the soul through all the divine notions, notions which are themselves transcended by that which is far beyond every name, all reason and all knowledge. Beyond the outermost boundaries of the world, the soul is brought into union with God himself to the extent that everyone of us is capable of it.[19]

Here, too, as with Moses' Sinai sojourn, the end or goal of the ascent past every name or word or knowledge is a union with God beyond

17. MT 5 1048B, 150.5–9, 141.
18. Not "befuddled," as I once put it too derogatorily or dismissively (*Commentary*, 213), as Peter Casarella rightly pointed out in his critical but fair review essay in the *Thomist* 59 (1995): 642f.
19. DN 13 981B, 230.1–5, 130. This (rather free) translation could have noted Phil. 2.9 for the name "above every name."

any and all affirmations and negations. The specific language used for "standing outside" one's natural domain has a long afterlife in the Christian tradition. As noted elsewhere, "ek-stasis" (ecstasy) carries several interrelated meanings within the Dionysian corpus.[20] At one point, our author uses this terminology to say "we should be taken wholly out of ourselves and become wholly of God."[21] Here, he describes how negations stand the soul outside its own conceptual limits, a hint of spiritual "ecstasy" to be developed by authors of later centuries, especially since the Areopagite's model on Mount Sinai could also be invoked.

At the curt conclusion of *The Mystical Theology*, the reader should also remember Moses at the end of chapter 1: in this darkness or cloud of unknowing, "being neither oneself nor someone else, one is supremely united to the completely unknown [God] by an inactivity of all knowledge and knows beyond the mind by knowing nothing."[22] The end or goal is union with God, but since it is a union beyond knowing and with the "unknown" God, no description is possible. The sudden silence seems intentional. In a hard-won recognition of the awe-inspiring transcendence of God, nothing more should or can be said.

20. See 130n266 of the Paulist edition, and *Biblical and Liturgical Symbols*, 137–38.
21. DN 7 865D, 194.12–15, 106.
22. MT 1 1001A, 144.9–15, 137, discussed above.

PART II

Stages of Dionysian Reception and Interpretation

1

The Doctrinal Concerns of the First Dionysian Scholiast, John of Scythopolis

Within a generation of their first recorded appearance, the Dionysian writings attracted the attention of an editor and commentator who added both an introduction and also (marginal) scholia to the corpus, influencing subsequent readers enormously.[1] Comprehensive treatment of the doctrinal concerns of the first Dionysian scholiast, John of Scythopolis (d. 548), would require full coverage of his *Prologue* to the Areopagite's works and of all his *Scholia* (somewhat over 550 comments, totaling well over 100 columns of text).[2] His

1. First published as "The Doctrinal Concerns of the First Dionysian Scholiast, John of Scythopolis," in *Denys l'Aréopagite et sa postérité en Orient et en Occident* ed. Ysabel de Andia (Paris: Études Augustiniennes, 1997), 187-200. © Institut d'Études Augustiniennes, by permission.
2. For an introduction and translation, see *Scholia*. The most important bibliography about John of Scythopolis and his work on the Dionysian corpus is by Beate Regina Suchla, as indicated below. For a quick sketch of John's life and work, plus general bibliography and an

central theological concerns, however, can be introduced by reference to a single brief scholion. Prompted by a cryptic phrase in the Areopagite's Letter 8, John declares that "By 'as a whole' he means the Lord who by taking both soul and body has saved us 'as wholes' [composed] of both soul and body."[3]

John's *Prologue* in defense of the orthodoxy and authenticity of the Dionysian writings indicates the areas of doctrine in question:

> But some dare to abuse the divine Dionysius with charges of heresy, being themselves absolutely ignorant of matters of heresy. For certainly, if they were to examine each of the items condemned among the heretics, they would discover that the teachings of these babblers are as far [from truth], as true light is from darkness. For what would they say of his theology of the only-worshipped Trinity? Or what about Jesus Christ, one of this all-blessed Trinity, the only begotten Word of God who willed to become fully human? Did he [Dionysius] not expound upon the rational soul and the earthly body like ours, and all the other items mentioned by the orthodox teachers? With what error could anyone rightly blame him, with respect to the intelligible and the intelligent and the perceptible things? Or, concerning our general resurrection which will happen with both our body and our soul? And concerning the future judgment of the just and the unjust?[4]

inquiry into selected scholia, see my article, coauthored with Lamoreaux, "John of Scythopolis on Apollinarian Christology and the Pseudo-Areopagite's True Identity," *Church History* 62 (1993): 469–82. Among earlier studies, see Hans Urs von Balthasar, "Das Scholienwerk des Johannes von Scythopolis," *Scholastik* 15 (1940): 16–38, as corrected and expanded in *Kosmische Liturgie: das Weltbild Maximus' das Bekenners*, 2nd ed. (Einsiedeln: Johannes-Verlag, 1961); and Bernard Flusin, *Miracle et Histoire dans l'oeuvre de Cyrille de Scythopolis* (Paris: Études Augustiniennes, 1983).

3. Awaiting Suchla's edition, the *Prologue* and the *Scholia* will be cited from *Patrologia Graeca* 4 by column and line number for the former and by column and the number of the scholion within its column (not the line) for the latter; in this case SchEp 545.8. Suchla's use of a Syriac translation (BM 12152, hereafter Syr) and early Greek manuscripts to identify John's scholia are explained in the introduction to the critical edition of Dionysius (38–54) and earlier in "Die sogenannten Maximus-Scholien des Corpus Dionysiacum Areopagiticum," *Nachrichten der Akademie der Wissenschaften in Gottingen I. Philologisch Historische Klasse* 3 (1980): 31–66. These publications indicate only the scholia on *The Divine Names*; using the same procedures, John Lamoreaux and I have tentatively identified (with the help of Saadi Abdul Masih) and translated from PG 4 John's scholia on all of the Dionysian corpus, as indicated in Rorem and Lamoreaux, "John of Scythopolis."
4. *Prologue*, 20 AB, cited in *Scholia*, 144–48; for a specific study of the text of the *Prologue*,

From this portion of the *Prologue*, we can summarize John's stated doctrinal concerns under four headings: the Trinity, Christ, creation, and eschatology. (This entire approach sets aside for treatment elsewhere John's concern for dialogue with Neoplatonism, whether the unacknowledged quotations from Plotinus or the open discussion of certain terms and concepts that stem in fact from Proclus.)[5] As amply documented in the *Scholia*, these four general topics yield two specific assertions over against certain heretics: given an orthodox doctrine of the Trinity, John affirms that Christ assumed an earthly body *and* a rational soul, against Apollinaris and his followers; given an orthodox doctrine of creation, he further affirms that humanity's final salvation is of the soul *and* the body, against all who deny the resurrection.[6] (Apollinaris, trying to affirm Christ's full divinity, thought that the divine Logos *replaced* the human mind of Jesus, thus compromising his full humanity.) The two convictions—incarnation in body and soul along with salvation of soul and body—complement each other and are occasionally found in tandem in his comments, as in the particular scholion chosen to begin this brief glimpse of John's doctrinal concerns.

In Letter 8, Dionysius rebukes a zealous and jealous monk named Demophilus with various scriptural testimonies of kindness and

see Suchla's "Die Überlieferung des Prologs des Johannes von Scythopolis zum griechischen Corpus Dionysiacum Areopagiticum," *Nachrichten der Akademie der Wissenschaften in Gottingen* 4 (1984): 176–87.

5. On John's surreptitious quoting of Plotinus, see W. Beierwaltes, "Johannes von Skythopolis und Plotin," in *Studia Patristica* 11.2, *Texte und Untersuchungen* 108 (Berlin: Akademie-Verlag, 1972), 3–7; and other studies noted in Rorem and Lamoreaux, "John of Scythopolis," n8. On the issue of John's dialogue with contemporary Neoplatonism, see H. D. Saffrey, "Un lien objectif entre le Pseudo-Denys et Proclus," in *Studia Patristica* 9, *Texte und Untersuchungen* 94 (Berlin: Akademie-Verlag, 1966), 98–105; Saffrey, "Nouveaux liens objectifs entre le Pseudo-Denys et Proclus," *Revue des Sciences philosophiques et theologiques* 63 (1979): 3–16; *Scholia*, 99–137.

6. All of these theological and philosophical concerns, along with John's sources and liturgical interests, are introduced in the general monograph and English translation of John's *Prologue* and *Scholia* by Lamoreaux and me in *Scholia*. For his partnership over our years of translating the scholia, writing the article cited above, and drafting the monograph mentioned, I am deeply indebted to Mr. Lamoreaux.

generosity, such as the splendid welcome of the prodigal son by his loving father. In applying Jesus' parable to Christ's own generous welcome of all who are penitent, the Areopagite uses a phrase that John found doctrinally marvelous. Loosely translated, it merely means "embracing them completely." One would hardly expect such a brief phrase among so many biblical examples to imply the orthodox doctrines of the incarnation and the resurrection. But this specific nomenclature has an anti-Apollinarian history before and after the Dionysian corpus and its *Scholia*—namely, in Gregory of Nazianzus and in John of Damascus. Dionysius had written "holos holous periphus" (ὅλος ὅλους περιφύς), literally, "whole embracing wholes."[7] In his well-known Letter 101, Gregory of Nazianzus wrote "so that the whole person, fallen because of sin, might be restored by a whole person, himself also God."[8] Although the Dionysian use of similar phrasing seems completely casual and rhetorical, far from any explicit christological context, our unknown author may well have known and here alluded to this anti-Apollinarian doubling of the word *whole*, namely, "the whole Christ saving the whole humanity." The compact formula became well-known later through John of Damascus, who combined it with another famous expression from elsewhere in Gregory's letter: "He in His entirety assumed me in my entirety and was wholly united to the whole, so that he might bestow the grace of salvation upon the whole. For that which has not been assumed cannot be healed."[9] The prehistory and posthistory of this terminology should not detain us very long from examining what John of Scythopolis made of it. But if the author of the Dionysian

7. Ep 8 1088A, 174.7, 271.
8. Ep 101, 15; PG 37 177C; SC 208, 42. SchEp 533.3 quotes this letter by Gregory, but the passage is not in the Syriac.
9. *Expositio fidei*, 3, 6; PG 94 1005B; *Die Schriften des Johannes von Damaskos*, ed. Bonifatius Kotter and pub. Byzantinischen Institut der Abtei Scheyern (Berlin: de Gruyter, 1981), 121. *The Orthodox Faith* (New York: Fathers of the Church, 1958), 280.

corpus did intend an apostolic invocation of this orthodox phrasing, then the scholiast was fully justified in seizing the opportunity.

In any case, John's scholion reveals much of his own theological position: "It is amazing how he says that [Christ] 'as a whole [embraces] them as wholes.' In this he puts to shame the heretics of that time, who used to say that only the soul is saved by God, not the body. By 'as a whole' he means the Lord who by taking both soul and body has saved us 'as wholes' [composed] of both soul and body. There were then heretics who followed Simon, as Irenaeus and Hippolytus indicate."[10] To John, the single word from Dionysius ("whole," singular and plural) teaches not only humanity's whole salvation including the resurrection of the body, as here asserted directly, but also Christ's whole incarnation including a rational soul, as implied here and as explicit in the *Prologue*. It was typical of Dionysius to allude to a biblical scene with a pithy and creative comment, whether or not it was intended to carry the weight of orthodox Christology, and typical of John to pile dogmatic weight upon a slender text. Our attention for the moment must remain on John and his doctrinal concerns.

In this scholion, John does not emphasize christological doctrine or heresies, but merely comments that the Dionysian word *whole* means "the Lord, having assumed soul and body." By itself, the phrase only hints at an anti-Apollinarian Christology, although the *Prologue* made explicit mention of a "rational soul." But there are many other scholia on this subject, including one that also makes a connection between the resurrection and Christology through the word *whole*. While discussing funerals and the placement of the body of the deceased, Dionysius comments on the resurrection: "Thus the

10. *SchEp* 545.8. The text goes on to say, "And those who teach the things of Origen also think the same things," but Suchla reports that this is not originally by John (personal correspondence, July 7, 1992). Nevertheless, as discussed below, John refutes Origen on this subject elsewhere.

whole person is sanctified . . . his whole salvation and his complete resurrection."[11] To this, John adds a remark that refers to another Dionysian text and invokes a well-developed Christology: "Note that by 'entire person' he means one composed of a rational soul and body, as is suggested by the expression 'in pure contemplation and understanding.' Note also that he refers to the 'whole salvation' of soul and body. One should pay careful attention to these two points so that you might understand the Incarnation of a rational soul and body when he elsewhere says that 'the transcendent Jesus wholly took on our human substance.'"[12] Here again John links soteriology to Christology through his holistic anthropology: as the whole person is saved including the resurrection of the body, so the whole person was assumed in the incarnation including the rational soul. In order to analyze these twin doctrinal concerns more closely, we here sever their linkage and treat them separately, as did John himself often enough.

Christology: "The Lord, Who by Taking Both Soul and Body . . ."

As suggested in the second scholion quoted above, John sees this anti-Apollinarian Christology "elsewhere" in Dionysius, and sometimes discusses it quite thoroughly including explicit refutation of heretics. (As quoted above, the *Prologue* shares this concern, although Charles Moeller exaggerated this concern somewhat in saying that "Tout le prologue est orienté dans le sense antiapollinariste.")[13] There are

11. EH 7 565C, 130.3–5, 257.
12. SchEp 181.17; "elsewhere" is DN 2 644C, 130.5–7, 63.
13. Charles Moeller, "Le Chalcédonisme et le néo-chalcédonisme en Orient de 451 à la fin du VIe siècle," in *Das Konzil von Chalkedon: Geschichte und Gegenwart*, ed. Alois Grillmeier and Heinrich Bacht, 2 vols. (Wurzburg: Echter, 1951), 1: 644n23. On sixth-century Christology in general, see Patrick T. R. Gray, *The Defense of Chalcedon in the East (451–553)* (Leiden: Brill, 1979); Alois Grillmeier, *Jesus der Christus im Glauben der Kirche*, vol. 2/2 (Freiburg: Herder, 1989); and other studies by Gray, Grillmeier, and others as cited in Rorem and Lamoreaux, "John of Scythopolis."

several direct references to Apollinaris and followers in the *Scholia*. At the very beginning of *The Divine Names*, Dionysius used the adverb "wholly" regarding the incarnation, prompting this from John: "See how he says that 'one of the hypostases wholly participated in us.' As the Apostle said, 'in him the fullness of the Deity dwells bodily.' The word 'wholly' is also contrary to Apollinaris."[14]

That Christ became "fully human," as already affirmed in the *Prologue*, is asserted in the *Scholia* explicitly over against Apollinaris. When the Areopagite summarized the Creed with a reference to Christ's "complete" sharing in humanity, John adds a quick comment: "against Apollinaris."[15] A campaign against the Apollinarian views condemned in the Council of Constantinople held in 381 may seem superfluous in the sixth century, except that various Apollinarian forgeries were still complicating the post-Chalcedon christological disputes. Indeed, John was known for his skill in detecting such forgeries, a facility that might lead us to other questions about authorship and forgery.[16]

The Dionysian texts and the comments by John must be seen against the background of the Council of Chalcedon itself. When Dionysius said that Christ was "utterly incarnate while yet remaining unmixed" (without confusion), John recognized the Chalcedonian opportunity, apparently added a longer phrase from the Formula, and opposed the arch-heretics by name: "And he [Dionysius] says 'utterly' [incarnate] since he took on both a rational soul and an

14. SchDN 196.4 on DN 592A, 113.7, quoting Col. 2.9. The opening part of this scholion (before the section quoted) is not in Syr, but its theopaschite ideas are confirmed in other scholia by John, as discussed below. Shortly after this scholion on the word "wholly," John claims (in SchDN 197.2) that the Dionysian phrase against the Apollinarians, that is, "the whole man" (cf. SchEH 181.17 quoted above), can thus be dated from the apostles, as can the Chalcedonian adverbs against the Monophysites, "without confusion" and "without change."
15. SchEH 144.14 on EH 3, 436D, 88.8–10.
16. Leontius of Jerusalem remarked that his neighbor and contemporary John had learned how to expose Apollinarian forgeries (*Contra Monophysitas*, PG 86 1856BC), as discussed regarding Dionysian authorship in Rorem and Lamoreaux, "John of Scythopolis."

earthly body. Rightly does he speak of an unconfused Incarnation, for when he appeared as a human, he remained God and preserved the properties of each of the two natures. Note also that this is against the Apollinarians."[17]

This direct quotation from the Formula of Chalcedon precisely where it echoes Leo's Tome, along with one explicit reference elsewhere to "two natures,"[18] could give the mistaken impression that John was a diophysite or Nestorian opponent of Apollinaris and all his offspring. But as a Chalcedonian, or rather a neo-Chalcedonian, John of Scythopolis opposed not only Apollinaris and Eutyches but also Nestorius and his cohorts. His is a well-balanced and nuanced Christology, one especially designed to portray the Dionysian writings as completely orthodox on this point. When Dionysius mentioned briefly that Jesus was "completely" among us, John expands the remark with a via media strategy:

> Note that God the Word alone became incarnate. He says that it [the incarnation] is "perfect," against Apollinaris, since it is from an intelligent soul and our body. This he makes clear by saying "according to us," which is also against Eutyches. It is also against Nestorius, because he speaks of "the unchangeable subsistence of Jesus" as God "according to us." Note also that he says that his mysteries in humanity are real [existent]: hunger, thirst, walking on the water, passing through closed doors to his disciples, raising the dead, the passion itself, etc.[19]

Here John has expanded significantly on the Areopagite's text and has revealed more of his own strategy. He opposes the Nestorians, here and elsewhere, with the flat assertion that Jesus is God, even if he must insert such a comment into this particular Dionysian passage.[20]

17. SchEH 149.15 on EH 3, 444C, 93.16–17. The middle sentence is not in Syr, presumably because the Syriac (Monophysite?) translator intentionally omitted John's clear allusion to Chalcedon.
18. SchCH 57.3.
19. SchDN 216.3 on DN 640C, 125.19–20.

On the other hand, he supplies concrete and anti-Monophysite examples of Jesus' humanity and passion.

John's opposition to the Nestorians and the Eutychians (under several names) is plain from a large number of scholia, some of them quite explicit in nomenclature. In the course of paraphrasing an anaphora, the Areopagite referred to the incarnation, which prompted John to comment: "Note the precision of his teachings, which is clear in a multitude of passages, and fighting all heretics. On the one hand, that God's providence for us was self-working means that God the Word was one and the same, not one in the other, as some rave with Nestorius. On the other hand, the phrase 'in a true sharing of all our properties, yet sinlessly' overthrows the Manicheans, the Eutychians, the Apollinarians, and the Acephalians, and all other heretics at once."[21] The very format of this scholion employs the Chalcedonian strategy of a mean between erroneous extremes: orthodox truth resides between, on the one hand, the Nestorian error of associating the human and the divine too loosely ("the one in the other"), and, on the other hand, the mistake of the "Monophysites," under several names, in not asserting Christ's full sharing of humanity. Many of John's christological scholia adopt this balanced format, some of them as briefly as possible: "Note that this is against the Nestorians and the Acephalians."[22] The Acephalians, originally the "headless ones" (without a patriarch), are almost always named with the Nestorians in such double condemnations.[23]

20. See also SchEH 132.2: "Note that Christ is God, against the Nestorians," and SchCH 57.2; SchEH 116.5, 181.10, and SchDN 225.3.
21. SchEH 149.2 on EH 3 441A, 91.10–12.
22. SchCH 57.3, SchEH 165.18, and SchMT 425.2; see also SchCH 72.5 and SchDN 197.6, as well as others quoted above or below.
23. Of the eleven times John names the Acephalians, he pairs them with the Nestorians ten times: SchCH 57.3, 72.5; SchEH 149.2, 165.18; SchDN 196.4, 197.6, 209.11, 221.8, 229.5; and SchMT 425.2. The exception is SchDN 397.2, where they are named alone.

Despite the frequency of this via media approach, John is not content to stay with Chalcedon. In the wider context of sixth-century christological disputes, John's own position is classically neo-Chalcedonian: he wants to retain the Formula of Chalcedon but to interpret it along the lines of Cyril of Alexandria, including the assertion that God the Word suffered, indeed was crucified for us, albeit in the Word's humanity, not divinity. John's theopaschite Christology (that God suffered) is known from other sources,[24] and it is explicit in the *Scholia*: "[Note] also that God the Word is in truth the one who suffered, that is, in the flesh."[25] Amid highly charged polemics, John is careful in his wording: "Jesus Christ, God the Word, suffered for our sakes in the flesh, but not in his divinity."[26] The strongest and most explicit statement along these lines may or may not be by John himself, but it is consistent with his other comments: "Here he [Dionysius] declares the economy, that one of the trinity suffered. Note that one of the hypostases participated in us wholly; and that he calls our Lord himself, Jesus Christ, [first] simple, then a composite which called our human lowness to return to him. Therefore, it is right for us to say that one of the holy Trinity was on the cross. This is contrary to the Nestorians and Acephalians."[27]

However, John's own theopaschite Christology must serve his subtle presentation of an orthodox Areopagite. He therefore stresses a particular part of this assertion, namely, that Christ, God the Word, truly suffered in Christ's concrete, complete, and particular human nature. This emphasis has already been noted;[28] it can also be seen in John's comments on the famous Letter 4 in that John supplies

24. See Rorem and Lamoreaux, "John of Scythopolis," 472–73.

25. SchDN 221.8; see also the beginning of SchDN 196.4, although not in Syr.

26. SchDN 360.7.

27. SchDN 196.4, from the opening section, which is not in Syr. Note the classical theopaschite formula, "unus ex trinitate passus est."

28. Regarding SchDN 216.3, discussed above.

specific instances of Jesus' humanity where Dionysius had given none.[29] There is a further and extraordinary example of this emphasis when Dionysius quickly mentioned the "thearchic weakness." John took this to mean the self-emptying of the incarnation, and he elaborated at extraordinary length on the poverty and the passion of Christ: the manger, the homelessness, the lowly companions, the shameful death between thieves: "the piercing of nails, the lance wound in his side, the slaps on the face, the spittings, the vinegar, the bitter drink, the crown of thorns, the mockery and laugher, the genuflections, the cheap funeral and the grave."[30] Dionysius never mentioned such things, but John wants the reader to know that the Areopagite's is an orthodox view of the incarnation on this point as well. In the end, John's doctrinal concern is not only for the obviously anti-Apollinarian part of the affirmation, that Christ assumed a rational soul, but also for the other side of the story, that Christ fully assumed and experienced a human body with its weaknesses and mortality. It was, after all, the Severians who had first cited Dionysius as an authority. In claiming the Areopagite as his apostolic witness, the neo-Chalcedonian bishop of Scythopolis would brook neither overemphasis on divinity nor underappreciation of Christ's humanity. According to John's holistic anthropology, Christ was "whole, for the Lord assumed soul and body."

Eschatology: ". . . Has Saved Us 'as Wholes' [composed] of Both Soul and Body"

In John's comment on Letter 8, quoted above, he was clear and forceful about the salvation of the body, although he did not there

29. SchEp 536.1 on Ep 4 1072C, 161.11, naming eating and grieving as proper to Jesus' humanity; see also SchEH 132.11, emphasizing Jesus' death far beyond the Dionysian text in question (EH 2 404B, 78.8).
30. From SchDN 236.10 (an entire column of PG 4; this portion is at 237A) on DN 681D, 141.10.

name it the resurrection. He claims that Dionysius opposed the heretics of his time, those from "Simon" (discussed shortly), who said that God saved the soul but not the body. The *Prologue*, as also quoted above, made the resurrection of the body an explicit point of doctrinal concern. John's scholia on the resurrection cannot compare with the quantity and complexity of his remarks on Christology, but they are sometimes lengthy and always of substantial doctrinal significance.[31] They are clustered in two places: *The Divine Names*' discussion of the name "life" and *The Ecclesiastical Hierarchy*'s treatment of funerals.

The sixth chapter of *The Divine Names*, entirely devoted to the name "life," prompted from John two major scholia on the resurrection. The Areopagite's central concern is the concept of life here and now, as the middle term in the Neoplatonic triad of being, life, and mind (chapters 5, 6, and 7 of *The Divine Names*, respectively). Although in this chapter Dionysius did not mention the resurrection explicitly, he did refer to an afterlife of immortality for our "mixed" nature as souls and bodies, and he directly condemned the "mad Simon." John's two comments on the passage make the most of this opportunity to affirm the resurrection of the body and to condemn heretics:

> It is amazing how he teaches all doctrines in a correct manner! In this passage, as he hands on the mode of the resurrection, he declares that we are a mixture. We are a mixture insofar as we are mortals composed of immortal soul and mortal body. He says, on the one hand, that we are partly rational souls; on the other hand, that we are wholes, of body and soul. He says that our bodies are immortalized in the resurrection, asserting that the dogma of the resurrection seemed unbelievable to antiquity, which is to say, to the foolish opinion of the

31. John's scholia on the resurrection are SchEp 545.8 and SchEH 181.17 already covered, SchDN 337.2 and 337.5 under discussion here, and SchEH 173.7, 173.8, 176.2, 176.3, and 176.4, to be considered shortly.

> Greeks, because they thought that the immortalizing of the matter was contrary to nature. Foolishness is called antiquity! Although the fact of the resurrection is beyond nature, that is, with respect to the present manner of life which is supported by nourishment and excretion and sicknesses, nonetheless, with respect to God, nothing is either contrary to nature or beyond nature, since he is himself the cause of every life.[32]

Note, first, that the scholion repeats the holistic anthropology already seen in John, that we are "wholes," of soul and body. Second, John uses and repeats the word "resurrection," thereby making explicit and central in his remark that which was implicit and peripheral in the Dionysian passage at hand. Third, John counterattacks the objections of "the Greeks," namely, that the resurrection of material bodies is contrary to nature.

Dionysius himself had condemned the "faulty arguments of the mad Simon," but without specifying what they were. The problem was not simony (Acts 8), but that Simon had apparently mounted an argument from the senses against the imperceptible Cause of all, implying that something was contrary to nature.[33] Building on Irenaeus, John here and elsewhere considers this a foolish argument against the resurrection of the body, and responds strongly. "[Dionysius] says that the arguments of Simon contradict our doctrine which says that our bodies will rise again and be granted immortality—insofar as the fact is contrary to nature. Some who spoke against Simon also refuted him concerning these things: Irenaeus, Origen, Hippolytus and Epiphanius. The great Dionysius, however, divinely put an end to what is said by Simon, viz., that the resurrection of bodies is contrary to nature. Since nothing is contrary to God, how is anything contrary to nature?"[34] The use of Origen among the patristic authorities who oppose Simon on this point

32. SchDN 337.2 on DN 6 856D, 191.15–16, reading with the variant "mixed" to match the Dionysian text.
33. DN 6, 857A, 192.8–9.

is problematic, given the occasions discussed shortly where Origen and his followers are condemned for following the mad Simon in denying the resurrection.[35] The specific counterargument used by John and implied by Dionysius, namely, that nothing is contrary to God, would seem quite unpersuasive to the Greeks, depending as it does on a prior belief in God and in the resurrection. Taken together, however, these two scholia provide a strong witness to John's doctrinal concern for affirming the resurrection of the body over against specific opponents.

Where Dionysius himself is explicit about funerals and the resurrection, John has even more to say about his concerns for eschatology. In the seventh chapter of *The Ecclesiastical Hierarchy*, the Pseudo-Areopagite offers his only substantive treatment of eschatology, specifically on the afterlife as pertains to funerals.[36] We have already noted one brief scholion on that chapter, one that links the funeral for a "whole person" to Christ "wholly" taking on humanity—that is, a rational soul and body.[37] John's fuller discussions occur in a handful of sequential scholia, all commenting on the same paragraph of the opening section as it itemizes and dismisses alternative beliefs about death in favor of the one orthodox viewpoint. Modern identifications of these mistaken viewpoints might vary, but John thinks that he knows who the Areopagite is talking about.

Concerning the death of sinners, and what the Greeks think happens

34. SchDN 337.5 on DN 6 857A, 192.8; John refers relatively often to Irenaeus (SchEH 176.4; SchDN 337.5, 377.1; and SchEp 536.5, 545.8, 573.7, and 576.3), less frequently to Hippolytus (SchDN 337.5 and SchEp 545.8), and only here to Epiphanius.

35. Perhaps John's point here is that Origen opposed Simon in general. Or, perhaps, the original text did not refer to Origen as one of the authoritative Fathers on this point, given John's vehement condemnations of him elsewhere on the same issue. But how can we explain someone later adding Origen's name?

36. On the Dionysian treatment of funerals, including patristic precedents, see the 1955 translation of *The Ecclesiastical Hierarchy* by Thomas Campbell, 202–13.

37. SchEH 181.17, discussed above.

> after death, whose opinions he sets out. The more irrational of them (among them Bias, not the Prienean but another one) confess that the soul is not immortal, but mortal and is dissolved in the same way as the body, and passes into non-existence. There are others among them who are more rational (like Plato and some others) who philosophize about an immortal soul and say that after death the body no longer subsists, and that for all eternity it never returns to the subsistence it had. For this is what he calls "once for all" which is to say, "never to subsist again." For they say that it is unworthy for the material to live forever with the soul, in that the soul alone exists immortally. There are also heretics who say these things in various ways, e.g., those derived from Simon Magus, Menander, Valentinus, and Marcion and Mani. Even now there are some who take their stand on the myths, not teachings, of Origen. See with whom they wish to be numbered, and what sort of absurd opinions these men attach to the blameless faith of the Christians, these men who are abominable to God and to right-thinking people.[38]

After his learned reference to an obscure Bias, John's comment on Plato (his only explicit reference in the *Scholia*) introduces the main target: those who deny the resurrection of the body, whether philosophers or heretics, ancient or contemporary. That the material body is unworthy of such treatment alongside the immaterial soul is the heritage of Gnosticism, stemming from Simon Magus and including Origen, according to John's adoption of the argument of Irenaeus. The heated reference to an apparently contemporary controversy with Origenists ("even now") helps to date John's *Scholia*, especially given the more detailed information provided shortly.

After a quick burst of biblical passages to support Dionysius on this point, John resumes and refines his critique of Origen:

> There were then certain heretics like Simon Magus and his followers who said that there will be an ethereal body for the souls. One must

38. SchEH 173.8. There seem to be four mistaken notions identified in the Dionysian passage: that our bodies experience a dissolution of being, that the body's linkage with the soul is broken at death, that bodies are linked with different souls after death, and that the afterlife has a material bliss.

> know that Origen too says the same thing in one of his writings. In others, he completely denies even this, teaching that the entire bodily nature passes into non-being. Read the things written against his views on the resurrection by Methodius the holy martyr and bishop of Olympus of Adrianopolis [*sic*] in Lycia, and by Antipater bishop of Bostros. And you will learn of his [Origen's] monstrous and foolish fables.[39]

This key scholion could lead us away from John's basic doctrinal concerns to his complex array of patristic sources and his apparently contradictory references to Origen. The unique references to Methodius and especially to Antipater may help us date John's work shortly after 537/538 when the latter was invoked in Palestine to oppose the Origenists.[40] The odd reference to Adrianopolis could signal a corrupt text; perhaps John had originally included in this list Ammon of Adrianopolis whose anti-Origen work *On the Resurrection* he had already cited explicitly.[41] As to the references to Origen, they are usually vehement condemnations of his speculative doctrines, as here discussed regarding the resurrection. Nevertheless, Origen can also be cited and used as a biblical scholar without any such critique, as Methodius does and as John does in both the *Prologue* and the *Scholia*.[42] Apart from these complications in examining John's sources, his basic doctrinal position is clear: any compromise regarding the resurrection of the body must be directly rejected as monstrous and foolish. The intensity of John's concern is apparent not only in the vehemence of his language but also in his unusual

39. SchEH 176.3.
40. On Antipater, see Cyril of Scythopolis's *Life of Sabas*, in *Kyrillos von Skythopolis*, ed. E. Schwartz (Leipzig: J. C. Hinrichs, 1939), 189.14–22.
41. SchCH 65.6; this scholion concerns the angels rather than the resurrection.
42. The *Prologue* mentioned Origen without any overtones of heresy (20CD); John apparently used Origen's *Hexapla* (SchMT 421.2); and one scholion invokes Origen's homily on *Lamentations* positively (SchEp 549.6). There is a similar mixed use of Evagrius by John: specific Evagrian texts are condemned (SchEH 172.11, the same two passages condemned in the Ecumenical Council of 553), even as John can also cite Evagrius positively (SchCH 76.7). Lamoreaux and I have considered these passages more fully in the monograph mentioned above.

recourse to patristic authorities to buttress his case against this particular heresy.[43]

Conclusion

John's theological convictions about Christ and the resurrection of the body are implicitly grounded in a holistic anthropology: Christ's incarnation applies to the whole person, soul and body; humanity's afterlife applies to the whole person, soul and body. His doctrinal concerns for Christology and eschatology are explicitly connected to each other in that both are essential to his soteriology: "The Lord, who by taking soul and body *has saved* us 'as wholes' [composed] of soul and body." Many of John's comments on the Dionysian corpus concern minute points of grammar, vocabulary, and biblical sources; some engage in a complex debate with contemporary Neoplatonism; a few involve intricate and unattributed uses of Plotinus to oppose Plotinian teachings.[44] Overall, John's agenda involves a subtle defense of the Dionysian orthodoxy and authenticity. Yet among the myriad items of terminology, philosophy, and Dionysian exegesis, the learned bishop of Scythopolis shows a fundamental concern for salvation itself. As a further example, whereas the Areopagite used Carpos's strange vision of the heavenly and the demonic at the end of Letter 8 to make a general point about hierarchical generosity, John adds a note of soteriological fervor: "From such may the Lord free us!"[45] In terms of the quantity of references, explicit soteriology is not dominant in the *Scholia*, but it does unite and even explain several of John's doctrinal emphases. Nor could any reader of the *Prologue*

43. John cites other fathers often enough, but not so persistently or pointedly against a specific heretic; he usually seems content to condemn them on his own. He furthermore associates Origen with the most famous of heretics, indeed the father of heresies, Simon.
44. See notes 4 and 5, above.
45. SchEp 557.3 on Ep 8, 1100B, 191.2. Here and elsewhere (SchEH 132.9 and 176.6) John freely mentions the devil, Hades, and Gehenna, which the Dionysian texts never name.

be surprised that John's theological emphases pertain to salvation. He there calls them "the doctrines of salvation" and his list of doctrinal interests, cited above, concludes with their soteriological significance: "To speak in short, our salvation is focused on these points, which it would not be right to go through in detail, since the exposition in the *Scholia* signifies all of these things at the proper time."[46]

As John deferred his detailed exposition of these points from the *Prologue* until the proper time in the *Scholia* themselves, so this brief chapter must defer the fuller exposition of many points to another context. Yet even an exhaustive analysis of John's work must honor his stated doctrinal concern for salvation: "By 'as a whole' he means the Lord who by taking both soul and body has saved us 'as wholes' [composed] of both soul and body."

46. *Prologue* 20B; "doctrines of salvation" at *Prologue* 17C. See *Scholia*, 144–48.

2

The Early Latin Dionysius

Eriugena and Hugh of St. Victor

Dionysius the Areopagite arrived in Latin Europe, specifically in Paris, not as the apostolic missionary destined for beheading and a brief miraculous afterlife but rather as an identifiable Greek manuscript destined for translation and a long life of exposition and appropriation.[1] After the initial reception of the manuscript, the two key contributors to the early Latin Dionysian tradition were John the Scot (Eriugena) in the ninth century and Hugh of St. Victor in the twelfth century, both of whom wrote commentaries on *The Celestial Hierarchy*. This chapter sketches how they interpreted the Areopagite, emphasizing key passages for each. Eriugena's translation of the *Corpus Dionysiacum* and his *Expositiones* on *The Celestial Hierarchy* exerted a tremendous influence on subsequent Latin readers, including Hugh, and even survived the condemnation of his

1. First published as "The Early Latin Dionysius: Eriugena and Hugh of St. Victor," *Modern Theology* 24:4 (2008): 601-614. Also published in *Re-thinking Dionysius the Areopagite*, ed. Sarah Coakley and Charles Stang (Oxford: Blackwell, 2009), 71-84. © the author.

masterwork, the *Periphyseon*. The Victorine, whose own Augustinian inclinations were largely untouched by his encounter with the Areopagite, nevertheless exerted a distinctive influence by (falsely) attributing to Dionysius the view that in our pursuit of God, "love surpasses knowledge." Together, despite their stark differences, they bequeathed a lively Dionysian tradition to the high medieval authors, scholastics and mystics alike.[2]

Eriugena

In the early ninth century, ambassadors from the Byzantine emperor to the Carolingian court of Louis the Pious were apparently aware of the Parisians' conviction that their patron Saint Denis, the beheaded martyr, was originally the Athenian Areopagite and author. Among the diplomatic gifts they bore in the 820s was a Greek manuscript of the Dionysian corpus, immediately deposited in the Abbey of Saint Denis in the care of Abbot Hilduin. Earlier versions of the life of Saint Denis/Dionysius were pulled together by Hilduin and amplified with summaries of the Areopagite's writings now literally in hand. Hilduin also directed a translation of the Dionysian corpus, reflecting the specific features of this one Greek manuscript, still extant, including its variant readings, omissions, and errors. The Greek Areopagite had become a Latin Parisian, martyred but with a long and influential life yet ahead of him.[3]

2. For the Pseudo-Dionysian corpus itself and a fuller sketch of its influence in the Latin Middle Ages, see *Commentary*, including the authorship question and conflation with Saint Denis on 14–18. For much more on Eriugena's interpretation of Dionysius, see *Eriugena's Commentary*, including the fuller context for the texts included in this chapter.
3. On this manuscript and Hilduin's translation, see *Eriugena's Commentary*, 21–46, and the bibliography mentioned there, especially Gabriel Théry, *Études Dionysiennes*, vol.1: *Hilduin, Traducteur de Denys* (Paris: Vrin, 1932). On Hilduin, see Marianne M. Delaporte, "He Darkens Me with Brightness: The Theology of Pseudo-Dionysius in Hilduin's *Vita* of Saint Denis," *Religion and Theology* 13 (2006): 219–46.

Within a short generation of Hilduin's labors, another translation—by an Irishman named John (Eriugena)—took over. Using the same Greek manuscript, paired this time not with a life of the saint but with a full exposition of his thought, Eriugena's translation of the whole corpus and his commentary (*Expositiones*) on *The Celestial Hierarchy*, along with his overall appropriation of Dionysian themes within his own formidable corpus, together constitute the first major Latin reception of the Areopagite.[4] Eriugena never said why he worked out a new translation so soon after Hilduin, by the middle of the ninth century. Modern readers often note John's deeper grasp of some Dionysian concepts, especially the apophatic appreciation for the transcendence of God, but Hilduin's translation was not so notably deficient by contemporary standards as to need immediate replacement. Although clearly fallible, it was serviceable enough.[5] The motivation for translating Dionysius anew more likely stems from Eriugena's independent and creative energies and his inclination toward Greek theological categories, including eventually Gregory of Nyssa and Maximus the Confessor, rather than from any compelling problems in Hilduin's version.[6]

Eriugena took up the challenge of not only translating the Areopagite but also incorporating Dionysian insights into his own philosophical theology, notably in his masterwork, the *Periphyseon*. Late in his career he also wrote the line-by-line commentary on the first Dionysian treatise in this manuscript, his *Expositiones*. Here John immediately goes to the heart of the Areopagite's whole corpus as

4. The commentary by Eriugena is *Expositiones in Ierarchiam coelestem Iohannis Scoti Eriugenae*, ed. J. Barbet, CCCM 31 (Turnhout: Brepols, 1975), and will be cited as Exp with chapter and line numbers, followed by page, with translations taken from the appendix to *Eriugena's Commentary*.

5. See Théry, *Études Dionysiennes*; and *Eriugena's Commentary*, 73, for an example.

6. Frequently, however, Eriugena's labors are explained by way of critiquing Hilduin. For a recent example, see L. Michael Harrington, *A Thirteenth-Century Textbook of Medieval Theology at the University of Paris* (Paris: Peeters, 2004), 1.

he sees it and as he incorporated it into his own thought. As often noted, the opening of *The Celestial Hierarchy* is not first of all about angels, but rather about God, about revelation, and about theological method in the broad sense including apophatic or negative theology. To Eriugena, the very first Dionysian sentence in the corpus, in chapter one of *The Celestial Hierarchy*, was the key. He first provides the original text in translation (as here in capitals): "BUT ALSO EVERY PROCESSION OF THE MANIFESTATION OF THE LIGHTS, MOVED BY THE FATHER, COMING FORTH INTO US EXCELLENTLY AND GENEROUSLY, LIKE A UNIFYING POWER, AGAIN FILLS US AND TURNS US TO THE UNITY AND DEIFYING SIMPLICITY OF THE GATHERING FATHER."[7] As he does throughout his *Expositiones*, Eriugena adds to his translation some specific comments about Greek words, in this case explanations of "moved by the Father" and "generously" and "fills." Next he gives a paraphrase, the "sense" of the passage: "Thus the sense would be: just as the procession of the divine illumination abundantly multiplies us into infinity, it enfolds and unites and restores us again to the simple unity of the gathering and deifying Father."[8] After paraphrasing the Areopagite, sometimes more than once, Eriugena usually goes on to add some exposition of his own, revealing his theological interests.

Here he considers the opening Dionysian sentence to reflect the heart of the Areopagite's whole corpus:

> Now I say this because almost the entire purpose of the blessed Dionysius through all these books is [first] about the infinite plurality of the multiplication of the highest good, subsisting in itself, into all things, which through themselves would neither exist nor subsist as good things, unless they were to exist and subsist as good things by

7. Exp 1.144–48, 4–5; *Eriugena's Commentary*, 78 and 184.
8. Exp 1.202–5, 6; *Eriugena's Commentary*, 79 and 185.

> participation in the one who is essence and goodness in himself, and then [secondly] about the leading-back and return again of this multiform plurality into the highest good itself, in whom the infinite plurality finds its goal and is one.[9]

Taking his cue from the opening of the Dionysian corpus, Eriugena here not only identifies the "entire purpose" of the Areopagite's corpus but also reveals his own deep appropriation of the Platonic tradition of "procession and return." The "Father's lights" are not only revelatory, as in the Dionysian quotation, but also creative, as the source of existence itself proceeding from God, and even salvific, in the return of all back to this unifying source. When Dionysius adds another apostolic testimony, Eriugena paraphrases this central thought yet again: "And he affirms this by apostolic testimony, saying: 'ALL THINGS ARE FROM HIM AND TO HIM, AS THE DIVINE WORD SAYS' [Rom. 11:36]. It is as if he said: On this account the divine power collects us and enfolds us toward the unity and deifying simplicity of the gathering Father, since all things proceed from this source and all things return to this same goal, as the holy apostolic saying testifies."[10] Using the explicit language of proceeding from and returning to the same source and goal, Eriugena here isolates the entire purpose (*intentio*) of the Dionysian corpus. His thorough appropriation of this dynamic of procession and return, *exitus* and *reditus*, descending pluralization and ascending unification, is evident in the structure of his own "summa" of philosophical theology, the *Periphyseon*, as often noted. The world's "macrohistory" is there framed as procession from God (creation) and return to God (salvation), explicitly "the procession of the creatures and the return of the same," or "the return of all things into the Cause from which they proceeded."[11]

9. Exp 1.205–12, 6; *Eriugena's Commentary*, 79 and 185.
10. Exp 1.212–18, 6; *Eriugena's Commentary*, 79 and 185–86.

Further, when Dionysius goes on to specify the enlightenment coming down from the Father as "ANAGOGICALLY ENVEILED BY A VARIETY OF SACRED VEILS," Eriugena's paraphrase applies this image of descending yet anagogical (uplifting) veils to specific Dionysian treatises:

> As if he were to say: the paternal providence and the ineffable concern of the divine love, for our salvation and return toward that which we deserted by sinning, has enveiled the ray, invisible in itself, in various sacred veils, for reasons of uplifting. And it has prepared a certain mode of appearance from these [veils] which are co-natural and proper to us, in order that he who cannot otherwise be comprehended might be comprehensible to us. There is a full treatment of these veils both in this book, which is *On the Celestial Hierarchy*, and in the following one which is entitled *On the Ecclesiastical Hierarchy*, and certainly in the third *On the Divine Names*. But if you ask, we shall preview a few things among the many for the explication of the current sentence.[12]

He then summarizes *The Celestial Hierarchy*, *The Ecclesiastical Hierarchy*, and *The Divine Names* under this general category of "veils," itself part of the larger conceptual framework of (downward) procession and (upward) return. The literary legacy here is enormous, first in the *Periphyseon* itself so evidently structured along these lines. Furthermore, even when the *Periphyseon* was criticized and condemned in the thirteenth century (its version of "procession" was too close to a pantheist emanation, and the "return" of all sounded like universal salvation), Eriugena's translation of Dionysius and his *Expositiones* on *The Celestial Hierarchy* nevertheless continued to circulate freely. When interpreters of Thomas Aquinas's *Summa*

11. John Scottus Eriugena, *Periphyseon*, *Patrologia Latina* 122:528D–529A and 638C; see also 688D and 741C–744A. See the modern edition by É. Jeauneau (CCCM 161–65) as used in *Eriugena's Commentary*. On "procession and return" in Eriugena, see *Commentary*, 171, and the bibliography cited there, especially the foundational study of Maïeul Cappuyns, *Jean Scot Érigène* (Louvain: Abbaye du Mont César, 1933).
12. Exp 1.373–84, 11; *Eriugena's Commentary*, 80–81 and 189.

theologiae debate its fundamental structure, noting his own use of Romans 11 ("From him and to him and through him are all things"), Eriugena's early Latin appropriation of Dionysius is never far away.[13]

Hugh

David Luscombe and Dominique Poirel have both scoured the historical record for any traces of interest in Dionysius after Eriugena in the ninth century and before Hugh of St. Victor in the twelfth, and they have found very little.[14] Between Eriugena and Hugh, only a few authors took any notice of Dionysius, but interest picked up in the twelfth century, especially in Chartres and Paris. Hugh's use of "the fathers" is complex: he completely appropriated the Augustinian tradition, usually without attribution; yet, in contrast to his contemporaries, he rarely amassed patristic citations.[15] The Areopagite was a special case. When Hugh in his *Didascalicon* itemized the fathers regarding Christian literature, such as Augustine or Eusebius, he largely quoted previous lists and decretals. But he added a sentence of his own on Dionysius: "Dionysius the Areopagite, ordained bishop of the Corinthians, has left many volumes as testimony of his mental ability."[16] Nothing more is said there about these writings, and there is no mention of Paris. In *De vanitate mundi*, however, the long narrative about Christian martyrs

13. On Thomas, see *Commentary*, 172–74.

14. David Luscombe, "The Commentary of Hugh of Saint-Victor on the Celestial Hierarchy," in *Die Dionysius-Rezeption im Mittelalter*, ed. Tzotcho Boiadjiev, Georgi Kapriev and Andreas Speer (Turnholt: Brepols, 2000), 160–64; Dominique Poirel, "Le 'chant dionysien' du IXe au XIIe siècle," in *Les historiens et le latin medieval*, ed. Monique Goullet and Michel Parisse (Paris: Publications de la Sorbonne, 2001), 151–76, now in Poirel, *Des symboles et des anges* (Turnhout: Brepols, 2013), 243–70.

15. See Dominique Poirel, "'Alter Augustinus—der zweite Augustinus': Hugo von Sankt Victor und die Väter der Kirche," in *Väter der Kirche*, ed. Johannes Arnold, Rainer Berndt, and Ralf Stammberger (Paderborn: F. Schöningh, 2004), 643–68.

16. Hugh of St. Victor, *Didascalicon* 4.14 (PL 176:787A); trans. Jerome Taylor (New York: Columbia University Press, 1961), 116.

starts with St. Peter and then explains: "Dionysius the Areopagite, accepting his mandate, penetrated Gaul," fought for the truth, and showed the power of life by carrying his head in his hands.[17]

These minimal allusions and the relative absence of Dionysius from Hugh's major works raise questions about his one work that was directly on the Dionysian corpus. Long and thorough, his only nonbiblical commentary, the Victorine's exposition of *The Celestial Hierarchy* became a major part of a twelfth-century surge of interest in Dionysius.[18] Yet why he originally took on the project is never fully explained. On the face of it, the work seems to have originated in lectures for novice students and at their request, as he says: "I said first off and I say again now, lest I lead you on in (false) expectation, that I took up your request regarding the 'Hierarchy' of Dionysius not to attempt a full scrutiny of the depths of these subjects but only to uncover the surface of the words and expose them to the light. For this [introduction] is first of all more suited for beginners, especially because we know that what we have undertaken for discussion is too great and beyond our possibilities."[19] Surely Paris students, whether Victorine novices or external scholars who moved about the area, knew that the Abbey of Saint Denis housed not only the bodily remains but also the literary legacy of its patron saint. It would not be surprising if they asked Master Hugh to introduce them to the local saint who was considered the first of the fathers. On the other

17. *De vanitate mundi*, PL 176:737A.
18. A modern edition is by Poirel, *Hugonis de Sancto Victore Opera III: Super Ierarchiam Dionysii*, CCCM 178 (Turnhout: Brepols, 2015). Besides the prefatory material in that volume, the major study on this entire topic of Dionysius and Hugh is Poirel's companion volume, *Des symboles et des anges. Hugues de Saint-Victor et le réveil dionysien du XIIe siecle* (Turnhout: Brepols, 2013). Some of Poirel's conclusions were previewed in earlier essays: "L'ange gothique," in *L'architecture gothique au service de la liturgie*, ed. Agnès Bos and Xavier Dectot (Turnhout: Brepols, 2003), 115–42; "*Hugo Saxo*: Les origines germaniques de la pensée d'Hugues de Saint Victor," *Francia: Forschungen zur westeuropäischen Geschichte* 33, no. 1 (2006): 163–74; and "Le 'chant dionysien.'"
19. PL 175:960CD.

hand, Poirel speculates that Hugh brought with him to Paris a deep familiarity with Dionysius from his own student days and may have initiated the project himself.[20]

Hugh's *Prologue*, although separable and in fact often separated from the *Commentary* itself, twice confirms that this project was for beginners, literally "for those who should be introduced" to Dionysius, and he there makes a rudimentary introduction.[21] In this complex *Prologue*, Hugh introduces Dionysius in one place as a "theologian and describer of the hierarchies," and elsewhere as a "theologian and narrator of the hierarchies."[22] By itself this duplication would not cause much attention, but the *Prologue* also duplicates quite redundantly both its specification that these "hierarchies" are three (the divine Trinity, the triadic angelic hierarchy, and the human counterpart) and also the explanation for why Dionysius starts with the angelic (*The Celestial Hierarchy*), proceeds to the human (*The Ecclesiastical Hierarchy*), and culminates with the divine (*The Divine Names*).[23] For this and other reasons, the *Prologue* seems to be a composite of introductory remarks by Hugh, perhaps written after the *Commentary* itself and surely assembled later, probably after Hugh's death. These and other textual questions must await Poirel's edition and further studies. For now, however, regarding the purpose of Hugh's *Commentary*, the *Prologue* confirms and amplifies the point that this is for beginners. However deep and difficult the Dionysian concepts may be, Hugh's first task is a "moderate, common, and simple explanation unto understanding.

20. Poirel, "*Hugo Saxo*," 173–74. If the particular variants in Hugh's Dionysian text, or perhaps some marginalia, match the German group of Dionysian manuscripts rather than the Parisian, this speculation would be confirmed and might even explain how Parisians (including Abelard and Suger) suddenly became interested in Denis in the early 1120s.

21. "introducendis," PL 175:928B, 931BC.

22. "theologus et hierarchiarum descriptor," ch. 2, PL 175:927C; "theologus et narrator hierarchiarum," ch. 3, PL 175:929C.

23. PL 175:929C/930C and 931C/932B.

Indeed perhaps this will be an explanation more fitting for those who are to be introduced" to such great material.[24] Hugh's patient way of presenting the entire Dionysian text first, passage by passage, and only then offering his own comments on specific words or word order and overall meaning, supports this view of his pedagogical plan, although such was also the pattern in Eriugena's commentary.[25]

Eriugena's *Expositiones* had already explained many Dionysian words and phrases in the Latin vocabulary used in his own translation. This Latin Dionysius was supplemented by some further comments on the original Greek text translated by Anastasius, the papal librarian.[26] Hugh knows this legacy of the Latin Dionysius and may even be subtly refuting Eriugena on some points, but he does not here mention him or any other commentator.[27] A comprehensive analysis of Hugh's commentary, noting his special emphases and relationship to Eriugena's work, is a separate full-length project. Here only a few general observations with limited examples can be offered. The work cannot be dated precisely and may have been revised over time, but it seems to stem from the middle portion of Hugh's career, perhaps starting a little before the midpoint, around 1125. As a mature author, Hugh's basic emphases were then already in place, yet this project could still influence his later writings. Such timing allows us to look both for Hugh's own imprint in his comments on Dionysius and also for a Dionysian imprint on Hugh's other works.

24. PL 175:931B.
25. See Barbet's introductory comments to Eriugena, *Expositiones*, x.
26. See the recent work on Anastasius in Harrington, *Thirteenth-Century Textbook*.
27. See Heinrich Weisweiler, "Die Pseudo-Dionysiuskommentare 'In Coelestem Hierarchiam' des Skotus Eriugena und Hugos von St. Viktor," *Recherches de théologie ancienne et médiévale* 19 (1952): 26–47; Jean Châtillon, "Hugues de Saint-Victor critique de Jean Scot," in *Jean Scot Érigène et l'histoire de la philosophie*, ed. Édouard Jeauneau, Goulven Madec, and René Roques (Paris: Centre national de la recherché scientifique, 1977), 415–31. I am grateful to Ralf M. W. Stammberger for a prepublication copy of his essay "*Theologus nostri temporis Ioannes Scotus*: Hugh of St. Victor's Assessment of John Scotus Eriugena's Reception of Pseudo-Dionysius," a paper given at the 2000 Maynooth meeting of the Society for the Promotion of Eriugenian Studies, forthcoming in *Irish Theological Quarterly*.

Going through Hugh's entire commentary line by line confirms the judgment of previous scholars such as René Roques and Roger Baron that Hugh is here an objective and faithful expositor of the Dionysian text, sometimes giving it his own spin but not forcing it into his own mold.[28] The whole point is to present the Areopagite's own words (in Eriugena's Latin translation) sentence by sentence, usually phrase by phrase, so that the students can become acquainted with this father's text on a basic level. Hugh's own *Didascalicon* insisted on a patient encounter with the "letter" of any text first, before going on to the deeper meanings. Outside of the *Prologue*, Hugh never interjects into the Areopagite's thought, for example, his early and prominent pairing of the works of creation and restoration, even when the Dionysian language of "procession and return" might suggest it, as in the first chapter of *The Celestial Hierarchy*. Similarly, when Dionysius interprets the scriptural presentations of the angelic ranks and their activities, Hugh presents this exegesis on its own terms, never importing his own hermeneutical pattern of a threefold sense: literal-historical, allegorical-doctrinal, and tropological-moral. The result of his fidelity to Dionysius is that the Victorine's commentary is minimally "Hugonian": very little salvation history, only faint traces of *conditio/restauratio*, no eschatology, nothing about Noah's ark, no use of allegory or tropology, very little on pride and humility outside of the (pointed) discussion in the *Prologue*.

There are a few obvious Hugonian touches, such as the brief mention of "the three eyes" and the emphasis on the angels as teachers.[29] Here Hugh appreciated the Dionysian emphasis on angelic

28. René Roques, "Conaissance de Dieu et théologie symbolique d'apres l 'In hierarchiam coelestem sancti Dionysii' de Hugues de Saint-Victor," in *Structures théologiques de la Gnose à Richard de Saint-Victor* (Paris: Presse Universitaires de France, 1962), 294–364; Roger Baron, "Le Commentaire de la 'Hiérarchie céleste' par Hugues de Saint-Victor," in *Etudes sur Hugues de Saint-Victor* (Paris: Desclée de Brouwer, 1963), 133–218.

29. The mention of the "three eyes" is from PL 175:975D/976AB.

mediation, for revelation is basically pedagogical.[30] Further, Hugh consistently interprets the Areopagite's texts about knowing (and unknowing) in terms of knowledge and action or love, including service to the neighbor, beyond the Dionysian warrant.[31] One prominent excursus, pursued below, puts love above knowledge in a decidedly non-Dionysian way. Finally, the Victorine grants the Areopagite's point about apophatic or negative theology, that God transcends our categories and language,[32] yet without ever applying it as rigorously as the Dionysian corpus does. In general, Hugh defers to Dionysius, patiently presenting the Areopagite's text phrase by phrase for the students' sake. In the end, he even apologizes if his own words have covered up the Dionysian wisdom, like mud on marble.[33] With all this deference to the apostolic authority, Hugh's *Commentary* is explicitly Hugonian only rarely, as in the excursus on love above knowledge presented below as a case study.

There is another side to the relationship of Hugh to Dionysius, the converse of his commentary not being decisively Hugonian: is the rest of Hugh's corpus somehow Dionysian? That is, how did this deferential encounter with *The Celestial Hierarchy* and the other "apostolic" writings by the Areopagite influence Hugh's thoughts and other works? Briefly, as others have also noted, Hugh's overall corpus does not show many distinctive Dionysian footprints, whether from *The Celestial Hierarchy* or in general.[34] As Poirel concludes, there are no sudden signs of Dionysian influence in

30. See Poirel's contrast of Gregorian and Dionysian angelology in "L'ange gothique."
31. Jong Won Seouh, "Knowledge and Action in Hugh of St. Victor's Commentary on the Dionysian *Celestial Hierarchy*" (Ph.D. dissertation, Princeton Theological Seminary, 2007).
32. PL 175:972C–978D, esp. 974AB–975A.
33. PL 175:1154C. On this text, and the other few where Hugh comments on his own commentary, see Dominique Poirel, "La boue et le marbre: le paradox de l'exegese du Pseudo-Denys par Hugues de Saint-Victor," revised as "Exposer le *Hiérarchie céleste*" in *Des symboles et des anges*, 293–333.
34. Luscombe, "Commentary," 173.

Hugh's corpus, no new vocabulary or specific themes or overall theological orientation.[35] True, a portion of this *Commentary*, specifically on how the communion elements both symbolize and also *are* the body and blood of Christ, was incorporated later into the *De sacramentis*.[36] Yet this isolated example comes from a tangent within Hugh's *Commentary*, perhaps as rebuttal to Eriugena, not a specifically Dionysian point.

Outside of his *Commentary* on *The Celestial Hierarchy*, Hugh shows no definite Dionysian imprint in his presentation of the angels. In *De sacramentis*, for example, he chooses to draw on Gregory the Great but does not use the specific triple triad of angelic ranks distinctive to the Areopagite. Nor does he even use the language of "hierarchy" outside of this work, although the possibility that the *Commentary* itself was dedicated to King Louis VII and was "friendly to secular power and monarchy" is worth exploring further.[37] Grover Zinn has seen the Areopagite's triad of "purification, illumination, and perfection" in the ark treatises, but the texts do not seem Dionysian enough to argue any real influence.[38] Even someone who comes to Hugh eagerly looking for tracks of the Areopagite will not find hard evidence. The Victorine's descriptions of specific sacraments and orders show no trace of *The Ecclesiastical Hierarchy*; his presentation of Moses and the cloud on Mount Sinai is completely independent of *The Mystical Theology*; *The Divine Names* makes no real difference

35. Poirel, "Le 'chant dionysien.'" Curiously, Poirel speculates from this absence of discernable Dionysian influence ("*Hugo Saxo*," 173–74) that Hugh must have been a subtle Dionysian all along, already incorporating the Areopagite's thought into his own even before coming to Paris. The alternative argument, suggested here, is that Hugh was never that deeply affected by the encounter with Dionysius.

36. PL 175:951B–953D in PL 176:465D–408A, *De Sacramentis* (Part Two, chapter 3, vi–viii). Hugh also gave a compact and influential definition of "symbol" at 941BC.

37. Luscombe, "Commentary," 171.

38. Grover A. Zinn, "*De gradibus ascensionum*: The Stages of Contemplative Ascent in Two Treatises on Noah's Ark by Hugh of St. Victor," in *Studies in Medieval Culture* 5, ed. J. R. Sommerfeldt (Kalamazoo, MI: Medieval Institute, 1975), 61–79.

in Hugh's doctrine of God or the divine names or attributes. The occasional nod to apophatic theology is more generic than Dionysian, as seen before this Areopagite in Augustine himself. Overall, Hugh reflects the Augustinian appropriation of Platonism, not a Dionysian one. Even with Eriugena's thoroughly Dionysian versions of theophany, "procession and return," and the anagogical thrust of the symbolic (especially the incongruous) in his *Expositiones*, which were well-known to Hugh, the Victorine remains relatively non-Dionysian.

In fact, Eriugena provides the decisive contrast, for his encounter with Dionysius left a deep and broad imprint on his thought and overall corpus. John the Scot became a Dionysian, but Hugh of St. Victor remained an Augustinian or, rather, was his own Victorine. Thus, the basic contours of his thought can be understood with minimal reference to Dionysian material.[39] One specific excursus will illustrate how Hugh could take the Dionysian text, as mediated through Eriugena, and make it his own, leaving an enormous legacy for Victorine spirituality and medieval mysticism generally. But in general, Hugh's Dionysian *Commentary* remains largely peripheral to his overall corpus.

A Case Study: "Love above Knowledge."

Commenting on a passage in the Dionysian *Celestial Hierarchy* regarding the angels, Hugh wrote some influential words: "Love [*dilectio*] surpasses knowledge, and is greater than intelligence. [God] is loved more than understood; and love enters and approaches where knowledge stays outside."[40] The context concerns the etymologies of the angelic designations "Seraphim" and "Cherubim." *The Celestial*

39. Such as my own introductory overview, *Hugh of Saint Victor*, where "Hugh and Dionysius" is an appendix, including some material from this chapter.
40. PL 175:1038D.

Hierarchy had carefully noted that the word *Seraphim* means "fire-makers or carriers of warmth," while *Cherubim* means "fullness of knowledge" or "carriers of wisdom." Dionysius discussed the angels, their names, and various angelic ranks frequently, and not only in *The Celestial Hierarchy*, and he here explicated the symbolism of fire quite fully: mobile, warm, sharp, and so on. But Dionysius never identified the seraphic fire as the fire *of love*. To Hugh, with his overall interest in fire, seen elsewhere as well, it was plain that the Seraphim's fire was, indeed, the fire of love: the fire of *love* is mobile, warm, sharp, and the like.

On this point, Hugh is himself adapting a long tradition in Latin exegesis. The deep background is represented by Jerome, Augustine, and Gregory the Great; the crucial discussion is by Eriugena. In Gregory's Gospel homilies, especially on Luke 15 and the lost coin, he discusses the angels, their various ranks and names, and the precedent set by the apostolic Dionysius. Three times he refers to the Seraphim and their fiery love as part of an exegetical commonplace. Yet, he never claims that this is the Dionysian understanding of the name "Seraphim" or of the angelic ranks. As noted already, Eriugena is the key to many aspects of the medieval appropriation and adaptation of Dionysius. In his translation of *The Celestial Hierarchy*, chapter 7 (the chapter and the translation used by Hugh), John accurately presents the various attributes of the seraphic fire—warm, super-burning, inextinguishable, and so forth—and does so without adding any references to charity or love. In his commentary, however, Eriugena poetically explains warmth as the warmth of charity, and fire as the ardor of love: "Their motion is 'warm' because it burns with the inflammation of charity and . . . 'super-burning' because the first hierarchy of celestial powers burns above all who come after them in love of the highest good."[41]

Ten times in a single passage, love (*caritas* or *amor*) is associated with fire—warmth, ardor, burning, or flaming. "The fire itself of the celestial Seraphim is . . . 'inextinguishable' because the divine love always burns in it."[42]

Eriugena provided Hugh with the linkage between the seraphic fire and love, but he did not argue that the Seraphim and love were thus higher than the Cherubim and knowledge. On the contrary, he discusses the various and apparently conflicting orders used by Dionysius such as that in *The Celestial Hierarchy*, chapter 6, where the thrones are first and the Seraphim last in the supreme triad. But in general, as Hugh pointed out, the Seraphim are the highest in the Dionysian hierarchy, especially in chapter 7 of *The Celestial Hierarchy*, where they are superior to the Cherubim, the bearers of knowledge. Thus armed with Eriugena's linkage of seraphic fire and love, Hugh came to this specific Dionysian text, wrote a long excursus, and left behind the influential conclusion that love is superior to knowledge as the Seraphim are higher than the Cherubim.[43]

Hugh's *Commentary* on *The Celestial Hierarchy* has several other smaller digressions, some of them sounding homiletical and usually on the same issue of love and knowledge,[44] but nothing as extensive as the long excursus at the beginning of chapter 7. A single Dionysian sentence about the name "Seraphim" received fully nine columns of Hugonian expansion in the familiar Migne edition.[45] Besides its length, this excursus is extraordinary for the way it begins and ends. After quoting the Areopagite's sentence on the Seraphim, Hugh first marvels at these words; they are so profound and divine, he says, that

41. Exp 7.139–43, 95.
42. Exp 7.170–174, 95.
43. See also Hugh's terse linkage of love and knowledge in his homilies on Ecclesiastes at PL 175:175D and 195C.
44. PL 175:1043D, 1062–1066C, 1118B–1119C, 1130B.
45. The sentence is found in CH 7, 205C, 162; PL 175:1038–44.

they must have been revealed to the one who penetrated the "third heaven" into the paradise of God. Thus, the authority of the apostle Paul is first invoked for special insights into the celestial heights as then passed on to his disciple Dionysius, who wrote down such amazing words for us.[46] The long discussion of love and knowledge that follows is finally concluded nine columns later by breaking off and starting a new book with an explicit admission: "long intervals require a new beginning."[47] Hugh then reorients the reader to the Dionysian passage at hand and finally moves on to the Cherubim and their "fullness of knowledge."

Within this mini-essay on fire and love, on love and knowledge, Hugh employs a complex exegetical strategy, as Grover Zinn has already explored. What is this fire, moving and warm and sharp? "If we have said that this is love [*dilectio*] perhaps we seem to have said too little, not knowing what love is. Whoever says love never says little, unless perhaps he speaks of a little love. Now this [author] did not wish to speak of a little love, who has said so many things of love. 'Mobile,' he says, and 'unceasing and warm and sharp and superheated.'"[48]

The fire of love, now applied to human longing, is mobile, warm, and sharp, in that order, as seen in Luke's road to Emmaus. "Walking and loving, igniting and fervoring, what were they saying about Jesus, whom they heard and yet did not know along the way?"[49] When the walking disciples felt their hearts burn within them, they had mobility and warmth but did not yet have the sharpness of knowledge. "Because, however, they loved first, then they knew,

46. PL 175:1036A; see also 1029C.
47. PL 175:1045A. This phrase has often been taken to mean a major gap, perhaps several years, in the writing of the Commentary; Baron, "Le Commentaire," 134–35; Poirel, *Livre*, 110.
48. PL 175:1037A.
49. PL 175:1037B; Luke 24, as discussed by Grover Zinn, "Texts within Texts: The Song of Songs in the Exegesis of Gregory the Great and Hugh of St. Victor," in *Studia Patristica* 25 (Leuven: Peeters, 1993), 209–15.

so that 'sharp' might be in love as also 'warm.' First 'warm,' then 'sharp.'"[50] The sharpness of love penetrates to comprehension. "This love . . . goes through and penetrates all things until it arrives at the beloved, or rather goes into the beloved. For if you do not go into the beloved, you still love externally, and you do not have the 'sharp' of love."[51] With this conjugal imagery we are ready for the *Song of Songs*, with the melting and entrance and embrace. "Therefore he himself will approach to you, so that you will go in to him. You approach him then, when he himself goes in to you. When this love penetrates your heart, when his delight/love reaches as far as the innermost [space] of your heart, then he himself enters into you, and you indeed enter yourself so that you may go in to him."[52]

It is in this context of the bridal couch that Hugh says, "This is not . . . a great love, unless it go through as far as the bridal chamber, and enter the room, and penetrate as far as the interior things, and rest in your innermost [space]."[53] Then comes the well-known passage quoted earlier: "Love [*dilectio*] surpasses knowledge, and is greater than intelligence. He [the beloved of the *Song*] is loved more than understood, and love enters and approaches where knowledge stays outside."[54] Hugh was rarely that interested in the apophatic, but the image of a threshold here is the end of knowledge and thus the beginning of *un*knowing. These angels "surround by desire what they do not penetrate by intellect."[55] The bridal chamber of love is beyond the realm of knowing, and thus later authors can associate it with the darkness of unknowing, whether the cloud of Mount Sinai or the dark night of the lovers' embrace. Bonaventure,

50. PL 175:1037C.
51. PL 175:1037D.
52. PL 175:1038BC.
53. PL 175:1038C.
54. PL 175:1038D.
55. PL 175:1041A.

of course, became the master of these poetic associations, but Hugh of Saint Victor's excursus opened the way for this influential turn of the Dionysian apophatic toward the Franciscan affective.

Yet, there is still more in Hugh's minitreatise, as he waxes rhapsodic on every Dionysian word about the seraphim: "warm, sharp, intimate," and so forth:

> Because of this kind of marvelous operations of love, he [Dionysius] has said so many things about it, in which he would perhaps have said everything, if everything could be said. Still, we fear that we may have been negligent or fastidious. It is hard for us regarding something so sweet to leave out anything that we have received, and again it seems reckless to us to add something that we ought not. What is love [*dilectio*], do you think? When will everything be said? Behold we called it itself "mobile and unceasing and warm and sharp and superheated and intent and intimate and unbending and exemplative and re-leading and active and re-heating and reviving." And this seems to be much, and perhaps even enough, except that other marvelous things still follow, I do not know whether they are even more marvelous. "Fiery," he says "from heaven, and purifying like a holocaust." Two things should be noted, because he calls it "fiery," and at the same time "of heaven." For there is also another "fiery" from earth, but it is not similar to that which is "fiery" of heaven.[56]

He goes on to speak of a purifying fire, as a purifying love, and so forth. As a whole, this tangential exposition by Hugh marks the decisive step in a Victorine succession (such as Thomas Gallus) and thus for countless later spiritual writers like the *Cloud* author, Ruysbroeck, and Gerson, not only that love surpasses knowledge in the human approach to union with God, but also that this insight stems from a higher celestial realm and from privileged apostolic revelation through the apostle Paul to Dionysius, for in the "third heaven" seraphic love is higher than cherubic knowledge.

56. PL 175:1044AB.

Conclusion

In sum, the *Commentary* seems peripheral to Hugh's corpus and major concerns. Yet, even if the rest of Hugh's works may have been minimally Dionysian, the attention he brought to the Areopagite's corpus, including his use of Eriugena's translation and the way he interpreted it, left a considerable legacy for Richard of St. Victor, Thomas Gallus, Hugh of Balma, Bonaventure, and many other medieval spiritual writers taken up elsewhere. In the thirteenth century, the Latin Dionysian corpus circulated as an "annotated Areopagite" in the sense that Eriugena's *Expositiones* and Hugh's *Commentary* were routinely attached to it.[57] The early Latin transmission of the Areopagite was a thin tributary of two main authors, the first under later suspicion and the second never deeply Dionysian, yet through them flowed a translation, two commentaries, and a model for reading diligently the first of the fathers, especially for spiritual guidance.

As suggested above, the main tributary for Hugh's claim of Dionysian warrant for the idea of love surpassing knowledge in the spiritual life was the later Victorine abbot Thomas Gallus.[58] Although Gallus has not been widely appreciated until recently, his work was explicitly credited by the famous author of *The Cloud of Unknowing*, who also paraphrased *The Mystical Theology* in this Victorine direction. In the opening chapter above, the *Cloud* paraphraser adds love or affection several times regarding the general advice and the

57. Hyacinthe François Dondaine, *Le corpus dionysien de l'Université de Paris au XIIIe Siècle* (Rome: Edizioni di Storia e Letteratura, 1953). See now Harrington, *Thirteenth-Century Textbook*. See also the essays by Isabel de Andia, especially on Hugh of Balma and his adaptation of the Victorine Thomas Gallus, in *Denys l'Aréopagite: Tradition et métamorphoses* (Paris: J. Vrin, 2006), 213–56.

58. The most compact and accessible introduction to Gallus is Boyd Coolman, "The Medieval Affective Dionysian Tradition," in *Re-Thinking Dionysius the Areopagite*, ed. Sarah Coakley and Charles M. Stang (Malden, MA: Wiley Blackwell, 2009), 85–102, first published in *Modern Theology* 24, no. 4 (2008).

specific example of Moses.[59] He even added a wholly new sentence after the opening paragraph of prayer: "For since all these things are beyond the reach of mind, therefore with affection above mind, insofar as I can, I desire to win them to me by this prayer."[60] Ever since the *Cloud* author's paraphrase, building on Gallus's own paraphrases, love has often been added to knowledge in the interpretation of Dionysius.[61] This interpretive move might be defended on the basis of references to (cosmic) love in *The Divine Names*, but love is strikingly absent from *The Mystical Theology* itself.

59. For the specifics, see *Commentary*, 221.
60. See *The Pursuit of Wisdom and Other Works by the Author of the Cloud of Unknowing*, trans. James Walsh (New York: Paulist, 1988), 75, discussed in *Commentary*, 221.
61. For a broader discussion, including some medievals such as Albert the Great and Meister Eckhart who did not conflate love and knowledge in this way, see the concluding chapter below and *Commentary*, 216–25. For much more on Albert and Thomas Aquinas, see Bernhard Blankenhorn, *The Mystery of Union with God, Dionysian Mysticism in Albert the Great and Thomas Aquinas* (Washington, DC: The Catholic University of America Press, 2015).

3

Martin Luther's Christocentric Critique of Pseudo-Dionysian Spirituality

Martin Luther's theological criticism of "that Dionysius, whoever he was" is well-known for its polemical vigor and long-lasting influence.[1] The specific critique in Luther's mature writings was not completely novel, however, for it stood in continuity not only with his own earlier viewpoint but also with some prior commentators on the Areopagite, both Latin and Greek. For him and for them, the crux of the matter was always Christ and him crucified.

Perhaps the best known of Luther's assaults on the Dionysian corpus is in *The Babylonian Captivity* of 1520. Here, the Reformer ridicules the "hodge-podge about angels in his *Celestial Hierarchy*," the idle liturgical allegories in *The Ecclesiastical Hierarchy*, and more:

1. "Dionysius ille, quisquis fuerit," in Martin Luther, *D. Martin Luthers Werke,* Kritische Gesamtausgabe, 73 vols., ed. J. F. K. Knaake et al. (Weimar: Herman Böhlaus Nachfolger, 1883–2009), 5:503.10–11; hereafter cited as WA. This passage is discussed below in its context. First published as "Martin Luther's Christocentric Critique of Pseudo-Dionysian Spirituality," *Lutheran Quarterly* 11 (Autumn, 1997): 291-307. © *Lutheran Quarterly*, by permission.

> But in his *Theology* which is rightly called *Mystical*, of which certain very ignorant theologians make so much, he is downright dangerous, for he is more of a Platonist than a Christian. So if I had my way, no believing soul would give the least attention to these books. So far, indeed, from learning Christ in them, you will lose even what you already know of him. I speak from experience. Let us rather hear Paul, that we may learn Jesus Christ and him crucified [1 Cor. 2:2]. He is the way, the life, and the truth; he is the ladder [Gen. 28:12] by which we come to the Father, as he says: "No one comes to the Father, but by me" [John 14:6].[2]

This famous indictment, itself immediately indicted in the 1521 *Judgment of the Paris Theologians*,[3] introduces the historical and theological questions of this study: Luther's earlier experience with the Dionysian corpus, the christological antidote he offers—namely, the Pauline theology of the cross—and its precedents in medieval and early Byzantine comments on the Areopagite.

To Luther, the "pernitiosissimus" (most pernicious) Dionysius may have seemed "plus platonisans quam Christianisans" (more Platonizing than Christianizing). Yet what did he mean by "Expertus loquor" (I speak from experience)? This cryptic reference could be taken as evidence that Luther had been quite positive at first about the Dionysian writings and only later came around to his critical stance. A later comment reinforces this hypothesis and underscores Luther's harsh judgment that the Areopagite's theology was pernicious and even pestilential: "Thus, they taught that humans can converse and deal with the inscrutable, eternal majesty of God in this mortal, corrupt flesh without mediation. This is their doctrine which is regarded as highest divine wisdom; I also was in that camp for some time, not without great harm to myself. I admonish you to shun like

2. Martin Luther, *Luther's Works*, American ed., 77 vols., ed. Jaroslav Pelikan, Helmut T. Lehmann, and Christopher Boyd Brown (St. Louis: Concordia Publishing House; Philadelphia: Fortress Press, 1955–), 36:109; hereafter cited as LW. WA 6:562.8–13.
3. WA 8:289–90.

the plague that 'Mystical Theology' of Dionysius and similar books which contain such idle talk."[4] Here, too, Luther sharply criticizes Dionysius, this time associating his audacity with Müntzer and the Anabaptists, and apparently regrets his own earlier enthusiasm.

From Luther's pungent criticism of the long-revered Dionysian corpus, using his own earlier experience as a prime example, one might draw a double conclusion about discontinuity—namely, that Luther's mature critique of Dionysian spirituality differs sharply from his initial endorsement and that this break represents a Protestant departure from the medieval and Byzantine support for the Areopagite's theological program. On both counts, however, this scenario of discontinuity is misleading. First of all, Luther's own theological assessment of the Areopagite has certain continuities from the very early writings to the end of his career. Furthermore, his specific doctrinal position regarding the Dionysian corpus was not unprecedented. We can glimpse variations on this theme in Bonaventure, the early Byzantine authority Maximus the Confessor, and all the way back to the very first annotator of the corpus, John of Scythopolis. Since the case for continuity within Luther's own lifetime has been made by others, this essay need only reinforce that argument with some examples and exposition.[5] An argument for

4. "Disputation of December 18, 1537," WA 39/1:389.21–390.5. The reference to Müntzer and the Anabaptists is at 390.10–12. See Karlfried Froehlich, "Pseudo-Dionysius and the Reformation of the Sixteenth Century," in *Pseudo-Dionysius: The Complete Works* (New York: Paulist, 1987), 44.

5. Regarding the earlier argument for discontinuity in Luther's views of Dionysius, see Walther Köhler, *Luther und die Kirchengeschichte nach seinen Schriften, zunachst bis 1521* (Erlangen: Fr. Junge, 1900), 289–99. Erich Vogelsang's influential essay argued for Luther's fundamental critique but did not probe its early history; "Luther und die Mystik," *Luther-Jahrbuch* 19 (1937): 32–54. Arguments for Luther's early criticism and thus overall consistency regarding the Areopagite have been advanced by Heiko Oberman, "*Simul gemitus et raptus*: Luther und die Mystik," in *The Church, Mysticism, Sanctification, and the Natural in Luther's Thought*, ed. Ivar Asheim (Philadelphia: Fortress Press, 1967), 20–59; and by Karl-Heinz Zur Mühlen, *Nos Extra Nos: Luthers Theologie zwischen Mystik und Scholastik* (Tubingen: J. C. B. Mohr, 1972), 51–66, 110–11, and 200–203. For a summary of these arguments, with a brief presentation of the pertinent texts, see Froehlich, "Pseudo-Dionysius and the Reformation," 41–44.

Luther's modest continuity with some Greek and Latin predecessors, however, is more original and thus more exploratory than definitive.

Luther's Consistent Critique

Luther's mature criticisms of the Dionysian corpus were largely signaled in *The Babylonian Captivity* (1520), as already sampled. The judgment that the Areopagite's *Celestial Hierarchy* is "his own fancy and very much like a dream" is confirmed in a 1526 condemnation of "what Dionysius dreamed up about the celestial hierarchy . . . and impudently wrote down as if he himself had seen it."[6] In the 1535–1536 commentary on Genesis, Luther says flatly that Dionysius "invents nine choirs" that are "nothing but idle and useless human ideas."[7] For Luther, the heavenly hierarchy may well have its internal order with precise distinctions between the angels, but we human beings, as Augustine freely admitted, do not know enough to debate such subtleties. Nor do we need to know such things, for our faith depends not on them but rather, as the apostle Paul says, on Christ our redeemer who is Lord over all angels, devils, kings, and princes.[8] The New Testament kept all its angelic beings firmly subordinated to Christ, and Luther dismisses all speculations about the angels in and of themselves in order to keep the focus clearly on salvation through faith in Christ.

The Babylonian Captivity's dismissal of *The Ecclesiastical Hierarchy* as idle speculation wherein Dionysius can "amuse himself with allegories without proving anything" is also repeated in the Genesis commentary of 1535–1536.[9] "Full of the silliest prattle" about the

6. LW 36:109; "somniis simillima," WA 6:562.7–8. "Quae somniat Dionysius de coelesti hierarchia . . . quae ita impudenter scribit tanquam ipse spectarit." WA 13:568.15–18; LW 20:26.
7. LW 1:235; "Fingit novem Choros . . . ociosas et futiles hominum cogitationes." WA 42:175.4–8; cf. WA 34/2:275–76.
8. WA 45:290–91, a sermon from 1537.

celestial and the ecclesiastical hierarchy, Dionysius has been wrongly granted a vast authority regarding subdeacons, exorcists, and so forth, even though "nowhere does he have a single word about faith or any useful instruction from the Holy Scriptures."[10] Here, too, the speculative—in this case, liturgical details—must give way to the biblical centrality of faith in Christ. Having advised others to "read the Fathers with discretion," Luther does so himself, and ridicules the Dionysian fantasies about the angels and liturgical life insofar as they distract us from what is central.[11]

Beyond such criticism of the two hierarchical treatises, the doctrinal battle was truly joined when it came to the negative theology of *The Mystical Theology*. In 1520 and in his later critique of the Dionysian corpus as a whole, Luther insisted on a radically different understanding of the apophatic, or negative theology. He might use the same term, but, crucially, what he meant by it was not a matter of affirmations and negations in general. Regarding Psalm 90, he wrote in 1534:

> Therefore Dionysius, who wrote about "negative theology" and "affirmative theology," deserves to be ridiculed. In the latter part of his work he defines "affirmative theology" as "God is being." "Negative theology" he defines as "God is nonbeing."
>
> But if we wish to give a true definition of "negative theology," we should say that it is the holy cross and the afflictions in which we do not, it is true, discern God, but in which nevertheless that sigh is present of which I have already spoken.[12]

9. LW 36:110; "ludens allegoriis suis, quas non probat." WA 6:562.16.
10. LW 1:235; "plenissimus ineptissimarum nugarum . . . Cum nusquam unum verbum de fide, de ulla sarae scripturae utili eruditione faciat." WA 42:175.3 and 12–13.
11. LW 1:61, regarding Dionysian optimism on free will versus evil.
12. LW 13:110–11. "Quare merito ridetur Dionysius, qui scripsit de Theologia Negativa et Affirmativa. Postea definit Theologiam affirmativam esse: Deus est ens, Negativam esse: Deus est non ens. Nos autem, si vere volumus Theologiam negativam definire, statuemus eam esse sanctam Crucem et tentationes, in quibus Deus quidem non cernitur, et tamen adest ille gemitus, de quo iam dixi." WA 40/3:543.8–13. Cf. WA Tischreden 1:302–3.

Just as *The Babylonian Captivity* dismissed the Platonic and pernicious Dionysius in favor of the Pauline and crucified Christ, so also this later passage ridiculed abstract (and Platonic) affirmations and negations in favor of a distinctively Lutheran definition of negative theology—namely, the theology of the cross. From 1520 onward, Luther's christocentric critique of the Dionysian version of negative theology was clear and forceful. But how does it compare with his earlier remarks?

As with so many aspects of the young Luther's theology, the question of his early perspective on Dionysius can be profitably posed to his 1513–1516 *Dictata* on the Psalms. For example, he says that the "darkness" that hides God (Psalm 18:11) can mean the enigma of faith, or that Christ is hidden in the church, in the Virgin, or in the sacrament of the Eucharist. Of Luther's alternative readings, however, two other interpretations receive the fullest statement:

> Second, because He dwells in an unapproachable light (1 Tim. 6:16), so that no mind can penetrate to Him, unless he has given up his own light and has been lifted up higher. Therefore blessed Dionysius teaches that one must enter into anagogical darkness and ascend by way of denials. For thus God is hidden and beyond understanding. Third, this can be understood as referring to the mystery of the Incarnation. For He is concealed in humanity, which is His darkness. Here He could not be seen but only heard.[13]

Luther's reference to Dionysius is within his application of the Pauline "unapproachable light," including the need for humility in giving up one's own illumination. The phrases "tenebras anagogicas" and "per negationes ascendere" show a firm grasp of Dionysian vocabulary. Thus, one possible meaning of God's darkness is, with Dionysius, that God is "absconditus et incomprehensibilis." Luther then immediately juxtaposes a different meaning of darkness as the

13. LW 10:119–20; WA 3:124.30–35.

mystery of the incarnation, namely, *absconditus* in humanity, not seen but heard. Dionysius, indeed "the blessed" Dionysius, is employed as an authority here, but only for an alternative reading, one dominated by Luther's own biblical exegesis and adjacent to a strong reference to the incarnate Christ.

Later in the *Dictata*, Luther again mentions Dionysius with reference to silence and to negative theology. The transcendent majesty of God means that not only every word but also every thought falls short: "This is the true Cabala, which is extremely rare. For as the affirmative way concerning God is imperfect, both in understanding and in speaking, so the negative way is altogether perfect. Therefore a frequent word in Dionysius is 'hyper,' for beyond every thought one must simply step into the fog [darkness]. Nevertheless, I do not think that the letter of this psalm is speaking about this anagogy. Therefore our theologians are too rash when they argue and make assertions so boldly about matters divine."[14] Again, Luther honors the transcendent hiddenness of God, beyond human words and thoughts, and links such humility with the mysterious "Cabala," although without indicating what he understood by that name. That God is "beyond" all concepts is a recognition of divine transcendence, which is contained in the Latin prefix *super-* as used to translate the Dionysian "hyper." Luther has rightly isolated a single prefix as a summary of the Dionysian anagogy or ascent into the divine darkness. Nevertheless, he goes on to say that such is not the point of the psalm and, furthermore, that "our theologians" are too audacious in their affirmations about God. Although Dionysius is not directly criticized, this passage is hardly an endorsement. In fact, in light of Luther's later critique of the Dionysian audacity in describing divine things, one might consider

14. LW 10:313; WA 3:372.16–21.

the Areopagite to be implicitly included here in the critique of "our theologians."

These two texts from the early *Dictata* are typical of several passages there and in the early lectures on Hebrews (1517–1519). Regarding darkness or silence or even "negative theology," Luther cited Dionysius without explicit criticism and yet within certain boundaries.[15] These citations need to be evaluated alongside other early passages where the subject matter is similar, even if Dionysius is not named. In his 1516 lectures on Romans, Luther comments on Paul's emphasis on access and peace "through our Lord Jesus Christ" (Rom. 5:1-2): "This also applies to those who follow the mystical theology and struggle in inner darkness, omitting all pictures of Christ's suffering, wishing to hear and contemplate only the uncreated Word Himself, but not having first been justified and purged in the eyes of their heart through the incarnate Word."[16] If the references to "mystical theology" and darkness were not enough to identify Luther's opponents as those who follow the Dionysian way, he shortly identifies this ascent as *per Anagogem*. In light of Luther's developing theology of the cross, the problem with this Dionysian version of darkness and mystical theology is plain: it seeks God without going through the incarnation and suffering of Christ. Well before the 1520 criticism of Dionysius by name, Luther has clearly articulated his christocentric critique of the Areopagite's mystical theology. This passage on Romans is not unique. The entire development of Luther's theology of the cross from 1514 to 1520 provides the context for this emphasis and evolving polemic.[17]

15. Zur Mühlen calls it "eine kritische Distanz" (*Nos Extra Nos*, 53–54). Froehlich says that although Luther used some of this vocabulary (e.g., darkness and negative theology), "he was uneasy about the Platonic content from the start" ("Pseudo-Dionysius and the Reformation," 43).
16. LW 25:287; WA 56:299.27–300.3. The phrase "per Anagogen" is at 300.5.
17. See the excellent recent discussion, especially of the 1519–1521 Psalms texts, by Hubertus Blaumeiser, *Martin Luthers Kreuzestheologie: Schlüssel zu seiner Deutung von Mensch und*

Luther's criticism of the "mystical theologians" such as Dionysius is developed further in his 1519–1520 *Operationes* on the Psalms. There he warns against the dangers of commentaries on *The Mystical Theology* and of the Dionysian work itself as the opposite of negative theology, namely, death and hell. Such speculation is an ostentatious form of knowledge, as if understanding such things made one a theologian. "A theologian is made by living, indeed by dying and being damned, not by understanding, reading and speculating."[18] Later in this same work, another pithy expression of the theology of the cross has its original context in Luther's critique of Dionysius. Citing the Song of Songs on the bride of Christ, Luther speaks for the bride/soul:

> I have been reduced to nothing and know nothing. Entering into darkness and the cloud, I see nothing. I live by faith, hope and love alone, and I am weak (that is, I suffer) for when I am weak then I am stronger. This leading the mystical theologians call going into the darkness, ascending beyond being and non-being. Truly I do not know whether they understand themselves, if they attribute it to [humanly] elicited acts and do not rather believe that the sufferings of the cross, death and hell are being signified. The CROSS alone is our theology.[19]

Here, as in the later comment on Psalm 90 quoted above, Luther contrasts the negative theology of the mystical theologians, the Dionysian and Platonic methodology regarding negations and affirmations in the abstract (God as being and nonbeing), with his "negative" theology of the cross. The last sentence, with Luther's own capitals for the whole word *cross*, has been used to indicate his overall *theologia crucis* before 1520, as in Alister McGrath's recent

Wirklichkeit, Eine Untersuchung anhand der Operationes in Psalmos (1519–1521) (Paderborn: Bonifatius, 1995), 91–110. Blaumeiser also nicely summarizes the voluminous literature on "*Theologia crucis* und Mystik" on 64–72.

18. WA 5:163.20–30; see also 187.23–27.
19. WA 5:176.27–33; also discussed in Zur Mühlen, *Nos Extra Nos*, 201–2.

book (yet, unfortunately, without any reference to Luther's polemical context of opposing the mystical theology of Dionysius).[20]

In summary, the pre-1520 references to Dionysius in Luther's works do not indicate some theological approval that was later in need of being revoked. On the contrary, Luther had sharp criticism early and late for the "mystical theologians" who advance the Dionysian agenda. Luther may have been reluctant to attack by name an apostolic father who was a disciple of the apostle Paul, but he was forthright enough about his theological objections to the Dionysian mystical theology. The change that does occur in Luther's works of 1519 and 1520 is not doctrinal but historical. In the *Operationes* on the Psalms just described, Luther makes his first openly skeptical comment on the identity of the objectionable corpus, "that Dionysius, whoever he was."[21] Precisely while he was writing this work on the Psalms, shortly before his harsh critique in *The Babylonian Captivity*, Luther faced a major choice of perspectives on Dionysius as an apostolic writer. John Eck took a great interest in this first-century authority for the Roman view of hierarchy and the sacraments; just before he opposed Luther on these issues at the Leipzig Disputation of 1519, he published his own major work on the apostolic Dionysius.[22] On the other hand, Erasmus's Greek New Testament of 1516 contained a note on Acts 17:34 that drew attention to Lorenzo Valla's arguments against apostolic authorship for the Dionysian corpus. As repeated in his 1519 work on Corinthians, Erasmus added the humanist insight that the Dionysian liturgical rites were too elaborate and developed for the first century.[23] Luther, in choosing Valla and Erasmus over Eck, a

20. Alister E. McGrath, *Luther's Theology of the Cross* (Oxford: Basil Blackwell, 1985), the heading on 1 and the (fifth) chapter title on 148.
21. WA 5:503.9–10.
22. On Eck, see Froehlich, "Pseudo-Dionysius and the Reformation," 42n39–41; and Scott H. Hendrix, *Ecclesia in Via* (Leiden: E. J. Brill, 1974), 230–31.

Dionysius "whoever he was" over an apostolic authority, became increasingly free to dismiss the Dionysian writings, whether on Eck's points of hierarchy and sacraments or on the "pernicious" *Mystical Theology*. Yet this freedom of historical polemics did not mean that Luther had a complete change of heart regarding Dionysian thought. Perhaps the comments in which he later appears to repent of an earlier involvement refer not to a specific attraction to Dionysius but to a general embrace of monastic spirituality. In his rhetorical repudiation of that history as the "chief of sinners," Luther may have exaggerated his own acceptance of the Dionysian corpus. At any rate, his extent texts show an apparent discontinuity of historical perspective and polemical freedom but a certain continuity in doctrinal opposition to the Dionysian theology before and after *The Babylonian Captivity*.

Luther and His Predecessors

This scenario of Luther's pre-1520 perspective is confirmed by his comments on the *Theologica Germanica*, which also serves to introduce the question of Luther's predecessors among Dionysian commentators. In 1516, Luther published a short version of this anonymous work of spiritual theology with his own brief preface. He hazards the guess that it is by Tauler, whose genuine works have a Christ-centered emphasis much to Luther's liking. Again, Luther invokes the apostle Paul's emphasis in 1 Corinthians on Christ crucified: as to the foolishness of God, "we preach Christ, a folly to the heathen but to those who are called, the wisdom of God."[24] When he published a fuller version in 1518, his longer preface also invoked

23. On Erasmus, see Froehlich, "Pseudo-Dionysius and the Reformation," 39–40; and E. N. Tigerstedt, *The Decline and Fall of the Neoplatonic Interpretation of Plato* (Helsinki: Societas Scientiarum Fennica, 1974), 28–31.
24. Bengt Hoffman, trans., *The Theologia Germanica of Martin Luther* (New York: Paulist, 1980), 42.

1 Corinthians and claimed historical precedents for the Wittenberg theology: "And, if I may speak with biblical foolishness: Next to the Bible and Saint Augustine no other book has come to my attention from which I have learned—and desired to learn—more concerning God, Christ, man, and what all things are."[25] Not that there is any mention here of Dionysius. But Luther's pre-1520 interest in German mysticism coheres theologically with his perspective on the Areopagite's corpus. As Tauler added an emphasis on Christ crucified to the more abstract Dionysian theology of Meister Eckhart, whom Luther did not cite, so Luther's own comments about the Dionysian mystical theology consistently add an emphasis on the cross of Christ. As in both prefaces to the "German theology," this supplement (or critique) usually included an allusion to Paul's comments on the foolishness and wisdom of God in 1 Corinthians.

In general, Luther understood himself and his emphasis on Christ crucified not as innovative but as firmly grounded in the Christian tradition, including medieval authors such as Bernard and Bonaventure. Early and late, he praised them both for their focus on the incarnation, calling Bernard the best preacher ever, even better than Augustine, because he preached Christ most excellently, with Bonaventure in second place.[26] Vogelsang connects this praise to the Dionysian question: "Indeed the emphasis on incarnation and cross in Bernard and Bonaventure gave Luther a bit of help along the way against the Areopagite."[27] Such a broad claim merely introduces a more specific inquiry into Luther's predecessors regarding Dionysius. Bernard, however, is not fully relevant here, for he showed no

25. Ibid., 54. In the fourth edition of *Luther's Theology of the Cross* (Minneapolis: Augsburg, 1976), Walther von Loewenich admitted that Luther and Tauler shared a perspective on Christ (221–22), over against his original portrayal of their fundamental differences (156).
26. WATr 3:n3370; see also WATr 1:n683 and WA 43:581.11.
27. "Ja, die Betonung von Menschwerdung und Kreuz bei Bernard und Bonaventura hatten Luther gar ein Stück Wegs Hilfe gegen den Areopagiten gegeben." Vogelsang, "Luther und die Mystik," 38.

interest in the Dionysian corpus at all.[28] But Bonaventure, building later on the foundations of Bernard's twelfth-century contemporary Hugh of St. Victor, makes major use of the Dionysian writings. On the specific point of the Dionysian darkness and negative theology, Bonaventure's famous *Itinerarium* ends with a passage worth comparing to Luther. After quoting *The Mystical Theology* regarding the "divine darkness," Bonaventure concludes: "Let us, then, die and enter into the darkness; let us impose silence upon our cares, our desires, and our imaginings. With Christ crucified let us pass out of this world to the Father."[29] As a good Franciscan, Bonaventure naturally would emphasize Christ crucified. But to do so as an interpretation of the "divine darkness" in *The Mystical Theology* is to supplement the Areopagite precisely where Luther aimed his critique. Neither darkness nor negative theology are ever linked to the cross of Christ in the Dionysian corpus. Bonaventure is not criticizing Dionysius here, but he is synthesizing the presumably apostolic negative theology with the Franciscan focus on the suffering Christ. Nevertheless, with such a conclusion to the *Itinerarium* (and in opening comments such as "there is no other path but through the burning love of the Crucified"), he provides us with a medieval precedent to Luther's perspective.[30] It is not clear that the Reformer himself took this or any comment by Bonaventure as precedent

28. On Bernard's lack of interest in Dionysius, see Edmond Boissard, "Saint Bernard et le Pseudo-Aréopagite," *Recherches de Théologie Ancienne et Médiévale* 26 (1959): 214–63. On Luther's considerable interest in Bernard, however, see "Saint Bernard of Clairvaux in the Devotion, Theology, and Art of the Sixteenth Century," the essay by Franz Posset in *Lutheran Quarterly* 11 (1997): 329–35; his recent article "Bernhard von Clairvauxs Sermone zur Weih-nachts-, Fasten- und Osterzeit als Quelle Martin Luthers," *Lutherjarhbuch* 61 (1994): 93–116; and the extensive bibliography cited there, especially Theo Bell, *Divus Bernardus: Bernhard von Clairvaux in Martin Luthers Schriften* (Mainz: P. von Zabern, 1993).

29. Bonaventure, *The Soul's Journey into God*, trans. Ewert Cousins (New York: Paulist, 1978), 116, citing John 13.1.

30. Ibid., 54. Regarding the centrality of Christ in Bonaventure, see Ewert Cousins, *Bonaventure and the Coincidence of Opposites* (Chicago: Franciscan Herald, 1978); and Zachary Hayes, *The Hidden Center: Spirituality and Speculative Christology in St. Bonaventure* (New York: Paulist, 1981).

for his christocentric critique, despite Vogelsang's claim. Although Luther knew Bonaventure and his *Itinerarium*, there is no evidence that the Scholastic doctor was an influence here. Yet he was an important predecessor nonetheless. What Luther abruptly attacked, Bonaventure smoothly filled in—namely, the Dionysian neglect of the incarnation and cross of Christ when it came to defining and explicating negative theology.

Although Bonaventure's linkage of Dionysian darkness to death and to Christ is not a direct discussion of negative theology but rather a masterstroke of poetic association, we find more sustained treatments of the multifaceted apophatic method in the early Byzantine commentators on Dionysius. For the Eastern Orthodox, the most important interpreter of Dionysius was the seventh-century theologian Maximus the Confessor. In general, Maximus took the Areopagite to be an apostolic authority and therefore orthodox and above critique. Nevertheless, Maximus occasionally supplemented the Dionysian system with more explicit Christian content, including what John Meyendorff has called the "Christological corrective."[31] On this point, Maximus is concerned not for the subtleties of post-Chalcedonian Christology regarding the two natures of Christ and their relationship, but rather for the more basic question of the role of Christ in salvation. The Dionysian emphasis on negative theology was a general method of approach to the unknowable God. For Maximus, as for the Cappadocian fathers by whom he interpreted the Areopagite, the apophatic insight served to focus our attention on God as revealed in Christ: "The knowledge of himself in his essence and personhood remains inaccessible to all angels and men alike and he can in no way be known by anyone. But St. John, initiated as perfectly as humanly possible into the meaning of the

31. John Meyendorff, *A Study of Gregory Palamas*, trans. George Lawrence (London: Faith Press, 1964), 133, 185–92, 201–10.

Word's incarnation, claims that he has seen the glory of the Word as flesh, that is, he saw the reason or the plan for which God became man, full of grace and truth."[32] Here, negative theology leads to Christology; the apophatic serves the incarnational. The divine may be utterly transcendent, says Maximus with the Cappadocians, *but* the Scriptures witness to the revelation of God in Christ incarnate.

Maximus thus reveals a fundamental difference with Dionysius; as in Bonaventure, this is not a critique, but it does partially parallel Luther's preoccupation. The premise of negative theology can have various applications. For Dionysius, appropriate recognition of the transcendence of God (in affirmations and negations and silence) leads inexorably to union with God and not, according to his basic conceptual scheme, to or through the incarnate Christ.[33] For Maximus and for Luther, recognition of God's ultimate transcendence leads the believer to God's self-revelation in the incarnation. Maximus repeats this point immediately after the passage just cited: "For it was not as God by essence, consubstantial to God the Father, that the only-begotten Son gave this grace, but as having in the incarnation become man by nature, and consubstantial to us, that he bestows grace on us who have need of it."[34] On this crucial point, Luther's emphasis on the incarnation has a precedent in Maximus the Confessor. Of course, significant differences remain between Maximus and Luther, the former emphasizing the

32. *Chapters on Knowledge*, II, 76, in Maximus the Confessor, *Maximus Confessor, Selected Writings*, trans. George C. Berthold (New York: Paulist, 1985), 14; hereafter cited as *Chapters*.

33. "Dionysius . . . mentions the name of Jesus Christ and professes his belief in the incarnation, but the structure of his system is perfectly independent of his profession of faith." John Meyendorff, *Christ in Eastern Christian Thought* (Washington: Corpus Books, 1989), 81.

34. *Chapters*, 164. For further texts and exposition, see the introduction to this volume by Jaroslav Pelikan, who concludes: "One of the most significant ways to identify the place of Maximus Confessor in the history of Christian spirituality, therefore, is to see him, in his role as an interpreter of Pseudo-Dionysius the Areopagite, as the one who turned apophatic theology and spirituality around, from the speculative nihilism that was the potential outcome of apophaticism back to a concentration on the person of Jesus Christ" (9).

incarnation itself as revealing the glory of God and the latter stressing the passion in particular in his theology of the cross. But both found the Areopagite lacking a linkage between the apophatic method and the incarnation.

The importance of Maximus as a Dionysian interpreter has been compounded by the traditional ascription to him of a major commentary that is actually the work of the sixth-century bishop John of Scythopolis. The Dionysian *Scholia*, explanatory marginalia and footnotes in the early manuscripts, are now finally separable into the original comments by John and the subsequent observations of various authors, including Maximus.[35] Coming within a single generation of the authorship of the Dionysian corpus itself, John's work laid the foundations for all subsequent interpretations of the enigmatic Areopagite. John's observations on Christ, the incarnation, and the cross are particularly interesting in this context. Dionysius mentions Jesus often enough, but John makes the most of his rare references to the death of Christ and to any form of christological weakness or suffering.[36]

For example, when Dionysius makes fleeting reference to the "divine weakness" that receives liturgical praise, John provided an extraordinarily long scholion with more scriptural citations than anywhere else in his entire commentary. What the Areopagite passed by in silence, here and in general, the commentator discussed in detail: condescension, flesh, poverty, servanthood, homelessness, and a "dishonorable death on a cross."[37] Luther once complained that those who follow the mystical theology prefer sheer darkness,

35. For the procedures of citing John's scholia, see part 1 above and the first essay in part 2.
36. For example, upon the rare Dionysian reference to the "thearchic death" of Jesus (EH 3, PG 404B, 78.70), John adds multiple scriptural references (SchEH 132.11). On the famous Letter 4, John adds SchEP 532.3–4. For the method of citing John's *Scholia*, see part II chapter 1 above, note 3 on p. 62 above.
37. SchDN 230.10, commenting on DN 7 681D, 141.10.

"omitting all pictures of Christ's suffering."[38] This could not be said of John's long comment on the brief Dionysian phrase, for he provides multiple pictures of the passion: "the piercings of nails, the lance wound in his side, the slaps on the face, the spittings, the vinegar, the bitter drink, the crown of thorns, the mockery and laughter, the genuflections, the cheap funeral and grave."[39] John then draws heavily on Paul's phrasing, such as "crucified in weakness" and "unto death, even death on a cross," especially the 1 Corinthians interpretation of the foolishness of God as the cross of Christ.

When Dionysius elsewhere discussed the wisdom and foolishness of God directly, John also made a comment, but this time the proportions are reversed; the Dionysian discussion is full and detailed while the scholion is a terse aside. The Areopagite used 1 Cor. 1:25 ("God's foolishness is wiser than human wisdom") to launch an important exposition of negative theology: "It is customary for the theologians to apply negative terms to God, but contrary to the usual sense of a deprivation."[40] In the Dionysian version of the apophatic method, the "foolishness" of God is a particular form of negation, that God is not wise on the human scale but rather "hyperwise" or more-than-wise. Dionysius may have ignored the adjacent Pauline reference to Christ crucified and may have seized instead on the language of wisdom and foolishness to discuss the general principles of apophatic theology, but John's scholia turn the reader's attention back to the incarnation and the cross. Here, the bishop of Scythopolis anticipated the concerns of Maximus, Bonaventure, and Luther. Furthermore, John recognized that "other fathers" did not apply the Pauline "foolishness" to the general method of negative theology. "Note," he says, "how the father understood the saying of the Apostle,

38. WA 56:299.29–300.1, LW 25:287, cited more fully above.
39. SchDN 236.10 at 237A.
40. DN 7 865B, 193.10, 105.

for Chrysostom and the other fathers understood it to apply to the cross.[41] Here, too, the commentator is not overtly criticizing the apostolic authority. Nevertheless, from our perspective we could include Luther and his christocentric critique with Chrysostom and the other fathers who, unlike Dionysius, understood the Pauline foolishness to mean the cross of Christ.

Conclusion

These passages from John of Scythopolis, Maximus the Confessor, and Bonaventure do not represent any sort of tradition in Dionysian interpretation, much less one known to Luther. None of them, including Luther, ever referred to any other as a predecessor on this particular issue, although Luther certainly knew Bonaventure on this general theme. Nor do these texts represent a substantial body of comments on the Dionysian corpus; these are stray and brief remarks by widely scattered authors. But they are sufficient to dispel the impression that Luther's critique was unique as some sort of Protestant innovation. The commitment that negative theology must be clearly linked to the incarnation and death of Christ was common to many who grounded their work in the apostle Paul. John of Scythopolis noted that Dionysius applied the Pauline foolishness of God to a general method of negations instead of to the cross, as Chrysostom and the other fathers had. Maximus the Confessor used the apophatic principle not to approach the unknowable God directly but to redirect attention to the revelation of God in the incarnate Christ. Bonaventure poetically associated the Dionysian darkness with the death of Christ crucified. Compared with them, Luther's critique is obviously different regarding historical identification, but it is parallel in his theological concern: "If we wish

41. SchDN 340.4.

to give a true definition of 'negative theology,' we should say that it is the holy cross."[42] That such varied authors—early Byzantines, a high medieval Franciscan, and Luther himself before and after his excommunication—should come independently to the same conclusion about the Dionysian corpus might suggest that it is a valid criticism. Those who share this christocentric critique of Dionysian spirituality, however, should not give Luther all the credit, just as those who think it unwarranted should not give him all the blame.

42. Luther's enduring significance for the contemporary discussion of this point is indicated by David Tracy: "All Christian theology today needs to read Luther again for rethinking" aspects of the hiddenness of God. Tracy, "The Hidden God: The Divine Other of Liberation," *Cross Currents* 46 (Spring 1996): 11. More recently, see Piotr J. Malysz, "Luther and Dionysius: Beyond Mere Negations," in *Re-Thinking Dionysius the Areopagite*, ed. Sarah Coakley and Charles M. Stang (Malden, MA: Wiley-Blackwell, 2009), 149–62; originally published in *Modern Theology* 24, no. 4 (2008).

4

Negative Theologies and the Cross

The Dionysian version of apophatic theology has attracted some recent attention, but it is not the only variation on that traditional theme.[1] So many postmodern theologians are busy retrieving "negative theology," with others labeling such retrievals as "misconstruals," that observers might be tempted to conclude that there was, or is, such a single thing as "negative theology." Having a convenient label can suggest that there was something, reified, corresponding to the name, and indeed *one* such thing. Yet anyone seeking a definition or just sampling the texts encounters a diverse array of premodern apophatic authors, a multiplicity of negative theologies. I here survey some of the diversity within the Christian tradition of negative theology and yet also favor one strand of that tradition relative to Christ, the incarnation, and the cross.[2]

1. First published as "Negative Theologies and the Cross," *Harvard Theological Review* 101:3-4 (2008): 451-464; reprinted in *Lutheran Quarterly* 23 (2009): 314-331. © *Lutheran Quarterly*, by permission.

The biblical starting points make this a commonplace. "My thoughts are higher than your thoughts," says Isaiah's Lord. The divine is *in*visible, *in*effable, *in*comprehensible; these are all negations, out of a recognition of divine transcendence. Early authors such as Justin, Ireneaus, Clement, and Origen of Alexandria all built on these biblical materials. God by definition transcends our words and concepts and capacities, such that all affirmations must be qualified and only negations are flatly true. So what? Or, rather, *then* what? Some theologians make significant moves after the negations, out of this apophatic awareness of the surpassing transcendence of the Infinite, but they make *different* moves, theologically, and those differences are my main theme here. In short, where do such negations lead?

All types of Christian negative theology, to start with their common ground, keep negations *connected*; they do not isolate some apophatic principle of God's transcendence as if it were an independent epistemological truth. Negations stay connected, first of all, to affirmations, for there is something to be negated, some content to work with; even negative prefixes are negations of some specific word. Secondly, the negations are closely connected to the biblical texts, the words and symbols of revealed Scripture, since both the negations and the words being negated are originally scriptural. Indeed, a biblical symbol or metaphor shows the interplay of affirmation and negation: the symbol is both like and *un*like God. Finally, these biblical negations stay connected to communities of faith, indeed liturgical communities. The Christian apophatic grows out of worshipping communities, not abstract inquiry. It is indeed a misconstrual of negative theology to consider the apophatic as if

2. With my thanks to Harvard Divinity School for the invitation and hospitality surrounding the Dudleian lecture on April 17, 2008. I am most grateful to Sarah Coakley for her specific critique, as partially reflected in this revised text.

it were a free-floating epistemological principle for individuals, to isolate it from the cataphatic, from its biblical origins, and from liturgical communities of faith.[3]

To explain how theological negations can lead to different outcomes, I here propose three categories: the progressive apophatic, the complete apophatic, and the incarnational apophatic. Each has a central biblical source, a Greek father, and later successors in Latin Christianity. How each finds echoes in modern or postmodern discussions is more than I can document here.[4]

The Progressive Apophatic

In his "Contemplation on the Life of Moses," Gregory of Nyssa develops a biblical narrative into an apophatic theology. Promised God's favor and presence, Moses wants to see God: "Show me your glory, I pray" (Exod. 33:18). But what does it mean "to behold" God? Is it really "face to face, as one speaks to a friend" (Exod. 33:11)? No, says the Lord, "I will make my goodness pass before you . . . but you cannot see my face" (Exod. 33:19–20). Moses is hidden in a rock, cleft for him; *after* God's glory passes by, he may look. "You shall see my back," says the Lord, "but my face shall not be seen" (Exod. 33:23).

Here Gregory advances a profound and influential interpretation. Moses does get to behold God, not the way he or we might expect, but with an apophatic twist. That Moses sees God's back or backside is neither inappropriately anthropomorphic nor absurdly crude in Gregory's reading, but calls for a spiritual interpretation, an uplifting

3. Negative theology has "both a grammar *and* a vocabulary . . . the positive vocabulary of saying," not just a grammar of *un*saying. Mark Burrows, "Words that Reach into the Silence: Mystical Languages of Unsaying," in *Minding the Spirit: The Study of Christian Spirituality*, ed. Elizabeth Dreyer and Mark S. Burrows (Baltimore: Johns Hopkins, 2005), 213.

4. But see Denys Turner, "Apophaticism, Idolatry and the Claims of Reason," in *Silence and the Word*, ed. Oliver Davies and Denys Turner (Cambridge: Cambridge University Press, 2002), 11–34, for links from some of these same premodern authors to various postmodern discussions.

or "anagogical" interpretation. Moses is being uplifted, ever higher, ceaselessly higher. As if on Jacob's ladder, says Gregory, Moses "continually climbed to the step above and never ceased to rise higher, because he always found a step higher than the one he had attained."[5] Reviewing the life of Moses, Gregory charts the Mosaic ascent and ceaseless desire to keep ascending, even to this bold request to behold God. Here negation is gently implied in rising above one's current level; stepping higher entails leaving the lower behind in a type of denial that is repeated over and over.

As high as Moses may climb, as many rungs as he attains and then leaves behind, "he is still unsatisfied in his desire for more."[6] Here Gregory's apophatic becomes explicit: "The characteristic of the divine nature is to transcend all characteristics; [it] transcends knowledge; the Divine is by its very nature infinite, enclosed by no boundary."[7] "This truly is the vision of God," says Gregory, "never to be satisfied in the desire to see him."[8] To see God's back instead of God's face is not to view a static image of a physical back but to engage in the dynamic process of following someone. It means to follow where God is leading, for "he who follows sees the back."[9] God is leading Moses still higher, ever higher, always leaving behind the lower steps in a progressive apophatic. "So Moses, who eagerly seeks to behold God, is now taught *how* he can behold Him; to follow God wherever he might lead *is* to behold God."[10] This kind of dynamic negative theology recognizes that God is always beyond our grasp, our concepts, and our words—a recognition accompanied not

5. Gregory of Nyssa, *The Life of Moses* (New York: Paulist, 1978), II.227; 114.
6. Ibid., II.230; 114.
7. Ibid., II.234–35; 115.
8. Ibid., II.239; 116.
9. Ibid., II.251; 119.
10. Ibid., II.252; 119.

by nihilistic despair but by the perpetual "hope [that] always draws the soul from the beauty which is seen to what is beyond."[11]

Thus, to see God's back is to follow God ever higher, a gentle form of the apophatic linked to Gregory by Jean Daniélou under the term "epektasis," or "perpetual progress."[12] This endless pursuit of the infinite and inexhaustible divine nature is what I am here calling the "progressive apophatic." Moses is the best biblical example, but Gregory also interprets the Song of Songs this way, and he weaves Christ into both narratives. The bride, like Moses, wants to see the Lover's face, but he passes by (Song 5:6), not to forsake her but rather to draw her toward himself. She advances "towards that which lies before her and by always going out from what she has comprehended."[13] Of course, once the Song of Songs enters the picture, the apophatic is more than knowing and unknowing; Gregory's theme of "epektasis" applies not only to progressive knowledge of God by unknowing but also to ceaseless desire and love for God. Negations thus lead to more negations, endlessly to ever "higher" negations. This kind of progress, a generic form of negative theology, was often linked to the apostle Paul's example of "forgetting what lies behind and straining forward to what lies ahead" (Phil. 3:13).

With such a broad biblical pedigree, no wonder that this theme surfaces in many later authors, Greek and Latin, with no necessary connection to Gregory of Nyssa although his work did enter the Latin world in the early medieval translation and appropriation by Eriugena. Bernard of Clairvaux and William of Saint Thierry, as a

11. Ibid., II.231; 114.
12. In general, see Jean Daniélou, *Platonisme et théologie mystique* (Paris: Aubier, 1944); more specifically, Bernard McGinn, *The Presence of God: A History of Western Christian Mysticism* (New York: Crossroad, 1994), 1:14. McGinn here calls Gregory's "the first systematic negative theology in Christian history."
13. Gregory of Nyssa, *Commentary on the Song of Songs*, trans. C. McCambley (Brookline, MA: Hellenic College Press, 1987), 218.

pair of examples, take up the theme of perpetual progress in the spiritual life; such progress is perhaps "epektetic," in McGinn's adjectival form, but it is minimally apophatic. For Bernard, the Pauline model of "striving ceaselessly" is largely an affair of the heart, endless desire rather than endless knowledge.[14] William of Saint Thierry combines the intellect and love most expertly; for him, the shared ascent of mind and heart is endless progress, perpetually leaving behind what has been known and loved: "Always to advance in this way is to arrive."[15]

Like his friend and soulmate Bernard, William usually applied this theme of endless progress to the desires of the heart. Yet, he can also isolate the apophatic point about unknowing and, indeed, he does so regarding Moses in Exodus 33, as already seen in Gregory. When Moses was told "you cannot see my face," this refers to the knowledge of the divine majesty, says William. "That knowledge is best known in this life by unknowing; the highest knowledge that a man can here and now attain consists in knowing in what way he does not know."[16]

There are many other authors, medieval and modern, who share an affinity for this way of emphasizing an outcome of negative theology, the "progressive apophatic" that recognizes God's transcendence and thus the limitations of human capacity. Emmanuel Levinas, for example, built on this tradition with explicit appreciation for Gregory of Nyssa.[17] To give Gregory the last word in this section: "More is always being grasped, and yet something beyond that which has

14. McGinn, *Presence of God*, 2:216.
15. McGinn, *Presence of God*, 2:260; William of Saint Thierry, *The Way to Divine Union* (Hyde Park, NY: New City, 1998), 95.
16. William of Saint Thierry, Meditation 7.7; *On Contemplating God*, Cistercian Fathers 3 (Kalamazoo, MI: Cistercian Publications, 1977), 137.
17. Emmanuel Levinas, "The Trace of the Other," in *Deconstruction in Context*, ed. Mark C. Taylor (Chicago: University of Chicago Press, 1987), 359. I owe this reference to a helpful conversation with Stacy Johnson.

been grasped will always be discovered, and this search will never overtake its Object, because its fund is as inexhaustible as the growth of that which participates in it is ceaseless."[18] No particular polemics have accompanied this benign outcome of apophatic theology, that negations lead to more negations without end, but other authors took Moses' ascent up Mount Sinai to another end, with more controversial results.

The Complete Apophatic

After the "progressive apophatic," here based on Gregory of Nyssa, the second expression of negative theology I propose is the "complete apophatic," starting with the Dionysian mystical theology. Our author knew the Cappadocian (and Alexandrian) tradition but artfully disguised his debts. Like Gregory, Dionysius in *The Mystical Theology* depicts Moses climbing higher and higher, as we have seen, leaving behind and thus denying the lower steps; negations lead to more negations, but after this temporary similarity there is a difference at the peak, in the darkness or cloud of unknowing. Insofar as the Dionysian Moses negates everything that is less than God, he completes his apophatic ascent and finds himself united with the "unknown" God in the end. Negations lead ultimately to union with God. Paul's sermon in Acts 17 indeed started with the "unknown God" and ended up converting the original Dionysius and Damaris.

As a whole, as introduced in part 1, the Pseudo-Dionysian writings convey a devout reverence for the transcendence of God in biblical terms. "We offer worship," opens *The Divine Names*, "to that of the divine which lies hidden beyond thought and beyond being. With a wise silence we do honor to the inexpressible."[19] What immediately

18. Translation of *Contra Eun* I, 291, 112 (15–20); PG 45 340D. See Deirdre Carabine, "Gregory of Nyssa on the Incomprehensibility of God," in *The Relationship between Neoplatonism and Christianity*, ed. Thomas Finan and Vincent Twomey (Dublin: Four Courts, 1992), 98.

follows, however, is not a wise silence by itself, or flat negation, but a complex engagement with Scripture according to an anagogical or uplifting interpretation that combines affirmation and negation: "With a wise silence we do honor to the inexpressible. We are raised up [uplifted] to the enlightening beams of the sacred scriptures, and with these to illuminate us, with our beings shaped to songs of praise, we behold the divine light, in a manner befitting us, and our praise resounds for that generous Source of all holy enlightenment, a Source which has told us about itself in the holy words of scripture."[20]

Dionysian apophatic theology, specifically in *The Mystical Theology*, could by itself leave the misleading impression of an isolated and abstract principle that God is flatly unknowable. On the contrary, as I have argued above, the Dionysian apophatic is paired with the kataphatic or affirmative theology in the interpretation of Scripture first of all.[21] The idea that negations about God are simply true whereas affirmations always need to be qualified is all about interpreting the Bible. Such symbols, like a cornerstone or the wind, are both like and *un*like God, and so are the human concepts that stem from such exegesis. This anagogical interpretation of "the enlightening beams of the sacred scriptures," furthermore, is not individualistic but communal, not abstract but concretely based on the Scriptures and the liturgy of the faith community. All three variations on the apophatic here proposed, including in this case Dionysius and soon Meister Eckhart, start with the positive contents of Scripture in Christian communities of faithful worship and praise for the transcendent God.

So, Dionysius, like Gregory, charts the progress of Moses through purification and illumination, as he sees and understands, up to

19. DN 1 589B, 111. 4-6, p. 50.
20. DN 1 589B, 111. 6-12, p. 50-51.
21. *Commentary*, 53–57 and 194–205, with other studies mentioned there.

perfection or union, but then there is a difference. Gregory's Moses never stops ascending, for his progressive apophatic is everlasting. The Dionysian apophatic, however, is not perpetual but completed in that Moses does arrive, and it is absolute in that by negating and surpassing everything that is not God, Moses ends up in God, united to God. To quote again the climax of this ascent: breaking free of what sees or is seen, Moses "plunges into the truly mysterious darkness of unknowing. Here, renouncing all that the mind may conceive, wrapped entirely in the intangible and the invisible, he belongs completely to him who is beyond everything. Here, being neither oneself nor someone else, one is supremely united to the wholly Unknown by an inactivity of all knowledge, and knows beyond the mind by knowing nothing."[22]

After all the biblical interpretation of the perceptible and the conceptual, in the liturgical context of a worshipping community, the finale of the Dionysian apophatic is union with God. In the end, negation and silence are the direct way to the unknown God, beyond words and thoughts. The apophatic is complete, not progressive, and in ecstatic eternity, not everlasting time. It is also radically complete, for God is finally "not wisdom nor one nor oneness, divinity nor goodness; it is not spirit or sonship or fatherhood."[23] Since *The Mystical Theology* has been discussed above, I leave Dionysius instead with a quotation from the end of *The Divine Names*. Following all of his philosophical interpretation of the biblical names for God, the Areopagite's longest treatise also turns apophatic, and with the same turn to ecstatic union with God. He agrees with the Scripture writers, he says, for

> their preference is for the way up through negations, since this stands the soul outside everything which is correlative with its own finite

22. MT 1 1001A, 144.10–15, p. 137.
23. MT 5 1048A, 149.8–150.1, p. 141.

> nature [i.e., renders the soul ecstatic]. Such a way guides the soul through all the divine notions which are themselves transcended by that which is far beyond every name, all reason and all knowledge. Beyond the outermost boundaries of the world, the soul is brought into union with God himself to the extent that every one of us is capable of it.[24]

The Dionysian apophatic culminates in union with God, beyond all affirmations and negations. Symbols and concepts, assertions with denials, have charted the way, but in the end they are all left behind. This variety of negative theology seeks and finds God by negating all that is less than the infinite God, including all finite words and concepts. No wonder that some later "mystical" theologians embraced the Dionysian form of negation, but only a few, for it is difficult to sustain the absolute apophatic by itself above and beyond the "progressive apophatic." Perhaps the best example, surely the best known, is Meister Eckhart.

Skipping many centuries and the thin Dionysian thread into Western Latin theology by way of Eriugena and Hugh previously covered, we come to a Dominican tradition of negative theology. Albert the Great is the key figure here, before Thomas Aquinas and his mountain of material, especially in Albert's commentary on the Dionysian *Mystical Theology*. Introducing the Areopagite's interpretation of Moses' ascent up and into the darkness of unknowing, Albert is rigorously apophatic. As to lights and sounds and words, "all these things have to be transcended, because none of them is what we seek in contemplation."[25] Albert maintains the Dionysian insistence that Moses is united with the utterly unknown God by knowing nothing, and he does so without here adding love to the pinnacle as the Victorines and Franciscans did.[26] Albert remains

24. DN 13 981B, 230.1-5, p. 130.

25. Albert the Great and Thomas Aquinas, *Albert and Thomas, Selected Writings*, trans. Simon Tugwell (New York: Paulist, 1988), 158, translation adjusted (461.19). See now Blankenhorn, *The Mystery of Union with God*.

completely apophatic right to the end of *The Mystical Theology*, where the "transcendence of him who is above all [even] transcends all negation. The names which are denied of him are denied because of his transcendence . . . [and] his transcendence defeats all negation."[27]

As launched by Albert and developed in Thomas, a Dominican trajectory then epitomized in Meister Eckhart applied the mendicant ideal of poverty to apophatic theology, not only owning nothing and wanting nothing but also "knowing nothing,"[28] in the special sense later called "learned ignorance." Eckhart very much liked and quoted the Dionysian caution about the "wise silence" that honors the inexpressible and the idea that negations are true whereas affirmations are unsuitable.[29] God is beyond all names and words, even "good" or "being," since God is beyond our understanding. If you have a God you can understand, goes the Augustinian saying that Eckhart passes on, that is not really God.[30] Specifically exegeting Exodus 33 and Mount Sinai's cloud, says Eckhart, "The meaning is then 'Moses went into the darkness wherein God was,' that is, into the surpassing light that beats down and darkens our intellect."[31] He quotes from the Areopagite's Letter 1, "Perfect ignorance is the knowledge of him who is over all that is known."[32] Here, echoing the Dionysian comments on Moses, is Eckhart's complete apophatic, which leads to the famous "breakthrough" into God beyond God, the sinking

26. McGinn, *Presence of God*, 4:23–24; see also my *Commentary*, 214–25, and the essay above on Hugh of St. Victor.

27. *Albert and Thomas*, 198.

28. Sermon 52, in Meister Eckhart, *Meister Eckhart: The Essential Sermons, Commentaries, Treatises, and Defense* (New York: Paulist, 1981), 199–203; hereafter *Essential Eckhart.*

29. *Essential Eckhart*, p. 280; Meister Eckhart, *Meister Eckhart: Teacher and Preacher* (New York: Paulist, 1986), 70; hereafter *Eckhart, Teacher.*

30. *Essential Eckhart*, 206–7. Augustine, "Si comprehendis, non est Deus," *Sermon* 117.3.5 (PL 38:663).

31. *Eckhart, Teacher*, 117.

32. Ibid., 118; Ep 1 1065B, 263.

into the nothingness of God. Love takes God wearing a garment—namely, God's goodness—but knowing and unknowing "peels everything away, and takes God bare," yet "can never encompass him in the sea of his unfathomableness."[33] With the "negation of negation," the apophatic is absolute, and that is how one breaks through to God, in the unfathomable sea. Angela of Foligno, Hadewijch, Mechthild of Magdeburg, and especially Marguerite Porete also spoke of the "abyss" in this way, as Amy Hollywood has pointed out.[34] "Abyss" itself is a negation (*a-byssum*), but as a negativity regarding dereliction or abandonment, as McGinn argues, rather than an apophasis about God per se.[35] To conclude with Meister Eckhart: here, too, as with Dionysius, negative theology is not an abstracted principle of language or religious epistemology, but rather a way of interpreting Scripture within the community of faith. This is clearer among the Byzantines, such as Gregory Palamas, but Eckhart's best expressions of this complete apophatic occur, after all, in his homilies, meaning that they are founded on biblical content and take place within a liturgical context.[36] In this respect, the postmodern contender for expressing a complete apophatic, namely, Jacques Derrida, was correct to distance himself from Dionysius and Eckhart because they held onto the biblical content within liturgical communities, whereas he wanted no such kataphatic baggage.[37] The Dionysian origins for this outcome of

33. *Eckhart, Teacher*, 254.
34. Amy Hollywood, *The Soul as Virgin Wife* (Notre Dame, IN: University of Notre Dame Press, 1995), 131, for Eckhart on "negation of negation."
35. Bernard McGinn, "The Hidden God in Luther and Some Mystics," in Davies and Turner, *Silence and the Word*, 103–10.
36. For Eckhart and Dionysius, see Bernard McGinn, *The Mystical Thought of Meister Eckhart* (New York: Crossroad, 2001), 177–78.
37. See especially the discussion between Derrida and Marion in Jean-Luc Marion, "In the Name, How to Avoid Speaking of 'Negative Theology,'" in *God, the Gift and Postmodernism*, ed. John D. Caputo and Michael J. Scanlon (Bloomington: Indiana University Press, 1999), 42–47, 68–70. Jeffrey Fisher argues for the compatibility of Derrida and Dionysius in "The Theology of Dis/similarity: Negation in Pseudo-Dionysius," *Journal of Religion* 81 (2001): 529–48.

negative theology (that negations lead to more negations *and* ultimately to union with God) immediately came in for some vigorous commentary on this apophatic point.

The Incarnational Apophatic

When Dionysius took his apophatic method to the extreme (stating that God is neither wisdom nor oneness, divinity nor goodness, neither Spirit nor Son nor Father), this was too much for some readers, including the first commentators, as introduced above. In the *Scholia*, or marginal comments attributed to Maximus the Confessor, we read: "Do not let this chapter disturb you and do not think that this divine man is blaspheming. His purpose is to show that God is not a being among beings but is beyond beings. For if [God] himself has brought forth all beings in creation, how can he be found to be one being among other beings?"[38] What then to do with this "apostolic" apophatic? Once one allows Dionysius to define the terms, as with most of the premodern tradition I am exploring here, one has limited the field considerably, as Grace Jantzen, Beverly Lanzetta, and other feminist theologians have rightly pointed out.[39]

The first commentator, John of Scythopolis, wanted to preserve some knowing amid the unknowing. Entering the darkness, "Moses in unknowing knew everything. . . . [Dionysius] explains here how God is known through unknowing."[40] Even *The Mystical Theology*'s final list of negations ("not spirit or sonship or fatherhood") is tempered by John's paraphrase in that he retains the name of "Trinity." "No one knows the pure *Trinity* as it is. . . . We do not

38. PG 4 429; of uncertain authorship: not by John of Scythopolis, perhaps by Maximus.
39. Beverly Lanzetta, "*Via Feminina* and the Un-saying of 'Woman,'" in *Radical Wisdom: A Feminist Mystical Theology* (Minneapolis: Fortress Press, 2005), 15ff.; Grace Jantzen, *Power, Gender, and Christian Mysticism* (Cambridge: Cambridge University Press, 1995), 109.
40. PG 4 421AB. See *Scholia*, 244.

know what the subsistence of the pure *Trinity* is, for we are not of its essence."[41] What John of Scythopolis does with specific Dionysian texts is fascinating but fragmentary, as glimpsed earlier in part 1.

A clearer example of turning the Dionysian apophatic to a different end, the third and final outcome for negative theology covered here, is the work of Maximus the Confessor. As hinted in the *Scholia*, Maximus interpreted Dionysius directly in his other works. To approach God "entirely above essence and entirely above thought," Moses enters the darkness of unknowing, "beyond the whole nature of the intelligible and the sensible realities."[42] But then what? Here is the decisive theological, or rather christological, move in applying the apophatic impulse. Yes, "no one has ever seen God," as Saint John says, but what then? Maximus makes his move, a decisive move, and it is not Dionysian:

> The knowledge of [God the Word] himself in his essence and personhood remains inaccessible to all angels and men alike and he can in no way be known by anyone. But St. John, initiated as perfectly as humanly possible into the meaning of the Word's incarnation, claims that he has seen the glory of the Word as flesh, that is, he saw the reason or the plan for which God became man, full of grace and truth. For it was not as God by essence, consubstantial to God the Father, that the only-begotten Son gave this grace, but as having in the incarnation become man by nature, and consubstantial to us, that he bestows grace on us who have need of it.[43]

In Saint John's terms, "No one has ever seen God. It is God the only Son, who is close to the Father's heart, who has made him known" (John 1:18). Negations thus lead to Christ incarnate.

41. PG 4 432B, *Scholia*, 248 (emphasis added).
42. Maximus, *Chapters on Knowledge*, II,82–83, in *Maximus the Confessor: Selected Writings* (New York: Paulist, 1985), 144.
43. Maximus, *Chapters on Knowledge*, II.76, 164; Andrew Louth, *Maximus the Confessor* (London: Routledge, 1996), 52–54.

Here the apophatic serves the incarnational, as in fact Paul's sermon in Athens starts with the unknown God and ends with the one raised from the dead. For Maximus, the apophatic recognition of God's transcendence does not lead to endless progress as in Gregory or directly to union with the unknown God as in Dionysius but rather to Christ as the incarnate revelation of God. Where the first outcome invoked endless time and the second featured ecstatic eternity, this third emphasizes salvation history. Of course, Gregory and Dionysius had their own Christologies, as various texts show, but their apophatic moves went in other directions, with other outcomes. Maximus is not critiquing Dionysius, the apostolic father, but his text supplements the Areopagite's with this direct link from negative theology to the incarnation. To put it flatly, because we cannot know God as transcendent, we look instead to God as incarnate. Dionysius never made that connection explicit. His negative theology never turns christological in *The Mystical Theology* or *The Divine Names*, and his comments on Christ, the incarnation, and the cross in *The Ecclesiastical Hierarchy* never turn apophatic.[44] There is one hint of the connection in Letter 3—"The transcendent has put aside its own hiddenness and has revealed itself to us by becoming a human being," yet it has remained hidden[45]—but this is never developed in Dionysius. It was Maximus who developed this linkage, moving from the apophatic about God's (immanent) transcendence to the kataphatic about God's (economic) incarnation. Where do negations lead? While Gregory featured "epektasis" or endless progress and Dionysius emphasized "apophasis" or absolute negation, Maximus

44. Ysabel de Andia has written eloquently on the Dionysian apophatic and on the cross in Dionysius, in "La théologie négative et la croix," in *Denys l'Aréopagite: Tradition et métamorphoses* (Paris: J. Vrin, 2006), 107–27. Yet she does not establish any direct linkage between the apophatic and the cross in Dionysius, in my judgment.

45. Ep 3 1069B, 264. I owe this qualification to the helpful critique of Charles Stang, whose book *Apophasis and Pseudonymity,* cited in part 1 above, develops a Dionysian apophatic anthropology in another way.

repeatedly turns to "kenosis," that the divine Word emptied itself into human likeness to the point of death, even death on a cross, as the apostle Paul says.

This variation on negative theology has many expressions; in the East, we would encounter the distinction between essence and energies or activities. The Western Latin tradition discussed here moves from a broad application of negative theology regarding the incarnation and human life in general to a specific focus on the mortality and death of Christ in particular. Bonaventure, for example, in the thirteenth century follows the Pauline kenosis from the divine down to the "human form" all the way to the "point of death," and he does so with an explicit move from the Dionysian apophatic to a Franciscan focus on Christ crucified. At the culmination of his classic work, *The Soul's Journey into God*, Bonaventure turns apophatic in his own way. Passing over into God in ecstatic contemplation, as Francis did, means that "all intellectual activities must be left behind and the height of our affection must be totally transferred and transformed into God."[46] Here Bonaventure has integrated love into unknowing, following the Victorine line discussed earlier. Yet there is more. He explicitly quotes *The Mystical Theology* at some length, noting that through the "ecstasy of a pure mind, leaving behind all things and freed from all things, you will ascend to the superessential ray of divine darkness."[47] Then the Franciscan makes the christological move from Moses and darkness to Christ, not merely to the incarnation of Christ but all the way to the cross. If you seek the Dionysian "superessential ray of the divine darkness," he suggests, you are entering the silent darkness of death with Christ crucified. "Whoever loves this death can see God because it is true beyond doubt that 'man shall not see me and live' [Exod. 33:20]. Let us, then,

46. Bonaventure, *The Soul's Journey into God* (New York: Paulist, 1978), 7.4; 113.
47. Ibid., 7.5; 115.

die and enter the darkness; let us impose silence upon our cares, our desires and our imaginings. With Christ crucified let us pass 'out of this world to the Father' [John 13:1]."[48]

The ending of Bonaventure's "Itinerary" is allusive and poetic and profoundly moving, far beyond these confines regarding negative theology. Nevertheless, with Maximus, Bonaventure turns the Dionysian apophatic to a christological proclamation. Moving beyond the Confessor's focus on the incarnation, the Seraphic Doctor stressed the culmination of the incarnation in the cross, following the Pauline "kenosis" to the end.

This specific outcome of negative theology, turning the apophatic to the crucified, is also represented by Martin Luther, as presented in the previous chapter. Like Maximus and Bonaventure, Luther knew well the negative theology of the Dionysian corpus. Unlike them, however, he did not revere this author as the Areopagite of Acts 17 and in fact quite openly ridiculed this Dionysius, "whoever he was," for his "hodge-podge" about angels, his idle liturgical allegories, and especially his dangerous teachings in *The Mystical Theology*.[49] "So far, indeed, from learning Christ in them [the Dionysian works], you will lose even what you already know of him. I speak from experience. Let us rather hear Paul, that we may learn Jesus Christ and him crucified [1 Cor. 2:2]."[50] Beyond this well-known critique in *The Babylonian Captivity*, Luther elsewhere speaks explicitly about "negative theology" and how it should turn us to the incarnation and the cross.

48. Ibid., 7.6; 116.

49. For more, see the previous chapter, "Martin Luther's Christocentric Critique of Pseudo-Dionysian Spirituality."

50. Martin Luther, *Luther's Works*, American ed., 77 vols., ed. Jaroslav Pelikan, Helmut T. Lehmann, and Christopher Boyd Brown (St. Louis: Concordia Publishing House; Philadelphia: Fortress Press, 1955–), 36:109 (hereafter cited as LW); Martin Luther, *D. Martin Luthers Werke*, Kritische Gesamtausgabe, 73 vols., ed. J. F. K. Knaake et al. (Weimar: Herman Böhlaus Nachfolger, 1883–2009), 6:562.8–13 (hereafter cited as WA).

Early and late in his career, he differs with Dionysius about Sinai's cloud or darkness of unknowing. To repeat from the very early *Dictata* on the Psalms: "Therefore Dionysius teaches that one must enter into anagogical darkness and ascend by way of denials. For thus God is hidden and beyond understanding. [Alternatively], this can be understood as referring to the mystery of the Incarnation. For He is concealed in humanity, which is His darkness. Here He could not be seen but only heard."[51] Here, early in his career, Luther makes the same point that Maximus made, turning from the darkness of the absolute God to the mystery of the incarnation in humanity.[52] Later, Luther went still further, not only in his bold critique of Dionysius but also in following the kenosis of an incarnational negative theology all the way to the cross, as with Bonaventure: "Therefore Dionysius, who wrote about 'negative theology' and 'affirmative theology,' deserves to be ridiculed. [In the latter part of his work] he defines 'affirmative theology' as 'God is being.' 'Negative theology' he defines as 'God is nonbeing.' But, if we wish to give a true definition of 'negative theology,' we should say that it is the holy cross and the afflictions [attending it]."[53] Here, of course, we are both repeating material from the previous chapter and also approaching too large a topic, Luther's overall "theology of the cross."[54] The only brief point at hand is how Luther explicitly turned from a Dionysian apophatic to a "negative theology" of the cross. The "mystical theologians," he writes elsewhere, may call going into the darkness "ascending beyond being and non-being," preferring to omit all

51. LW 10:119–20; WA 3:124.32–35.

52. See also Luther's comment that "inexperienced monks rise into heaven with their speculations and think about God as He is in himself. From this absolute God everyone should flee who does not want to perish." LW 12:312; WA 40/2:329.

53. LW 13:110–11; WA 40/3:543.8–13.

54. See also Vitor Westhelle, *The Scandalous God: The Use and Abuse of the Cross* (Minneapolis: Fortress Press, 2006). In the fourth edition of his classic *Luthers theologia crucis* (Munich: C. Kaiser, 1954), W. von Loewenich's new "Afterword" reconsidered how Luther's theology of the cross related to prior traditions of mysticism (245–48).

pictures of Christ's suffering, but, he says rather emphatically, "The CROSS alone is our theology."[55]

When Luther said, "Let us rather hear Paul," he meant the apostle Paul's foolishness of the cross, that God is not so much "unknown" as "hidden" in Christ. That Dionysius had applied 1 Corinthians instead to a general statement about negations was already a concern to the Areopagite's first commentator, as presented above. In writing "Note how the father understood the saying of the apostle, for Chrysostom and the other fathers understood it to apply to the cross," John of Scythopolis did not suggest that Dionysius neglects the cross in general but pointed out that the Areopagite did not here move from foolishness/wisdom to Christ crucified.[56] Thus, with "the other fathers" who turned negative theology to the cross, we should regard Luther as continuing the Pauline concerns of John the scholiast, Maximus the Confessor, and Bonaventure the Franciscan in this third use of the apophatic.

Yet Luther goes further still, and uncomfortably so for apophatic theologians. "Negative theology" does not lead neatly to the cross; it is actually opposed to the cross. Insofar as any negative theology seeks to manage God, it glorifies the self and is thus condemned by the cross. Negative theology can be all about our self-analysis, our recognition of the infinite, our epistemology, what we can and cannot know, but the cross is about God's "kenosis," the infinite in the finite, the divine soteriology, what God has done and will yet do. Further, for Luther, this christological turn is not simply a safe approach to God through the crucified, some successful albeit indirect access to the transcendent God after all. God preached is hidden and revealed in Christ, but the God not preached remains hidden, beyond our theological strategies.[57] Discourse about negative theology and

55. WA 5:176. 27–33. Cf. WA 56:299.27 to 300.3; LW 25:287.
56. *Scholia* 340.4 on DN 865B, *p.* 226.

the cross is not the point; for Luther, a theoretical theology of the cross is futile. What matters is when the word of the cross kills and makes alive again. The bad news for negative theology, Luther insists, is that the incarnate one died because we tortured and killed him, we who are not God and who are indeed opposed to God.[58] "You have become his betrayers and murderers," said Stephen (Acts 7). Luther's negative theology of the cross turns first of all to the condemnation of the law, the active proclamation of judgment unto repentance, and then to the gospel. When God's word of and on the cross destroys our theologies, apophatic and otherwise, then true faith in God is born.

Summary

To be simplistically kataphatic about it, there are at least these three outcomes for negative theology from the premodern tradition. First, a perpetual or "progressive apophatic" keys off Exodus 33, with Moses ever advancing morally and spiritually by following God in everlasting time. Negations lead to more negations. Second, a "complete apophatic" understands Sinai's darkness of unknowing in Exodus 19 and 20 as mystical union with God in ecstatic eternity. Negations lead to union with God. Third, an "incarnational apophatic" explicitly turns from such darkness, following John 1 and Philippians 2, to the incarnation and cross of Christ in salvation history. Negations about God as transcendent lead to faith in God incarnate and crucified. Gregory of Nyssa taught "epektasis," followed by William of St. Thierry and many others; Dionysius taught an "apophasis" of union, followed by Meister Eckhart and

57. David Tracy uses and advances Brian Gerrish's categories of Hiddenness I and Hiddenness II, in "The Hidden God; The Divine Other of Liberation," *Cross Currents* 46 (1996): 5–16.

58. LW 42:10; G. Forde, *On Being a Theologian of the Cross* (Grand Rapids, MI: Eerdmans, 1997), 3, 8.

very few others; Maximus the Confessor taught the Pauline "kenosis," which was taken further by Bonaventure to the death of Christ and still further by Martin Luther. There may have been other types or better examples; there are surely different apophatic moves possible today.

What moderns and postmoderns make of all this, I leave to others to discern, with just a few suggestions. Emmanuel Levinas and others echo the progress of Moses following God. Jacques Derrida wanted a complete apophatic but distanced himself from Dionysius and Eckhart for their linkage of the apophatic to the (biblical) kataphatic and to the (liturgical) community of faith. In modern theology, the classical orthodox tradition of Maximus, apart from the Latin Bonaventure and the Protestant Luther, has been represented ably, even beautifully, by Hans Urs von Balthasar.[59] May his eloquence, and these few lines about negative theology, lead more readers to Maximus the Confessor as an alternative form of negative theology alongside Gregory of Nyssa and the Dionysian mystical theology.

59. Besides his direct expositions of Maximus, such as *The Cosmic Liturgy* (San Francisco: Ignatius, 2003), see the eloquent little "elucidation" on "The Unknown God," in Hans Urs von Balthasar, *Elucidations*, trans. John Riches (London: SPCK, 1975), 18–25.

Bibliography

Primary Texts

Albert the Great, and Thomas Aquinas. *Albert and Thomas: Selected Writings.* Translated by Simon Tugwell. Classics of Western Spirituality. New York: Paulist, 1988.

Aristotle. *The Categories. On Interpretation. Prior Analytics.* Translated by H. P. Cooke and Hugh Tredennick. Loeb Classical Library 325. Cambridge, MA: Harvard University Press, 1938.

Augustine. *Sermo CXVII.* In vol. 38 of *Patrologia latina*, edited by J.-P. Migne, 217 vols. Paris, 1844–1864.

Bonaventure. *The Soul's Journey into God.* Translated by Ewert Cousins. Classics of Western Spirituality. New York: Paulist, 1978.

Cyril of Scythopolis. *Life of Sabas.* In *Kyrillos von Skythopolis*, ed. Eduard Schwartz, 85–200. Texte und Untersuchungen zur Geschichte der Altchristlichen Literatur 49/2. Leipzig: J. C. Hinrichs Verlag, 1939.

Eckhart, Meister. *Meister Eckhart: Teacher and Preacher.* Edited by Bernard McGinn. Classics of Western Spirituality. New York: Paulist, 1986.

———. *Meister Eckhart: The Essential Sermons, Commentaries, Treatises, and Defense.* Translated by Edmund Colledge and Bernard McGinn. Classics of Western Spirituality. New York: Paulist, 1981.

Gregory of Nyssa. *Commentary on the Song of Songs*. Translated by C. McCambley. Archbishop Iakovos Library of Ecclesiastical and Historical Sources. Brookline, MA: Hellenic College Press, 1987.

———. *Contra Eunomium libri duodecim*. In vol. 45 of *Patrologia graeca*, edited by J.-P. Migne, 162 vols. Paris, 1857–1886.

———. *The Life of Moses*. Translated by Abraham J. Malherbe and Everett Ferguson. Classics of Western Spirituality. New York: Paulist, 1978.

Hildegard of Bingen. *Scivias*. Edited by Adelgundis Führkötter. In *Corpus Christianorum Continuatio Mediaevalis* 43:1–2. Turnholt: Brepols, 1978.

Hugh of St. Victor. *De vanitate mundi*. In vol. 176 of *Patrologia latina*, edited by J.-P. Migne, 217 vols. Paris, 1844–1864.

———. *Didascalicon: A Medieval Guide to the Arts*. Translated by Jerome Taylor. New York: Columbia University Press, 1961.

———. *Hugonis de Sancto Victore Opera III: Super Ierarchiam Dionysii*. Edited by Dominic Poirel. In Corpus Christianorum, Continuatio Mediaevalis 178. Turnhout: Brepols, 2015.

Hoffman, Bengt, trans. *The Theologia Germanica of Martin Luther*. Classics of Western Spirituality. New York: Paulist, 1980.

John of Damascus. *Saint John of Damascus: Writings*. Translated by Frederic H. Chase Jr. New York: Fathers of the Church, 1958.

———. *Expositio Fidei*. In *Die Schriften des Johannes von Damaskos*, vol. 2, edited by Bonifatius Kotter and published by Byzantinischen Institut der Abtei Scheyern. Patristische Texte und Studien. Berlin: De Gruyter, 1973.

John of Scythopolis. *Scholia Corpus Dionysiacum IV/1, Ioannis Scythopolitani prologus et scholia in Dionysii Areopagitae librum "De divinis nominibus" cum additamentis interpretum aliorum*. Edited by Beate R. Suchla. Patristische Texte und Studien 62. Boston: De Gruyter, 2011.

John Scottus Eriugena. *Expositiones in Ierarchiam coelestem Iohannis Scoti Eriugenae*. Edited by J. Barbet. Corpus Christianorum, Continuatio Mediaevalis 31. Turnhout: Brepols, 1975.

——. *Periphyseon: Editionem nouam a suppositiciis quidem additamentis purgatam, ditatam uero appendice in qua uicissitudines operas synoptice exhibentur.* Edited by Édouard A. Jeauneau. Corpus Christianorum, Continuatio Mediaevalis 161–65. Turnhout: Brepols, 1996–2003.

Leontius of Jerusalem, *Contra Monophysitas.* In vol. 86 of *Patrologia graeca*, edited by J.-P. Migne, 162 vols. Paris, 1857–1886.

Luther, Martin. *Luther's Works.* Edited by Jaroslav Pelikan, Helmut T. Lehmann, and Christopher Boyd Brown. 77 vols. St. Louis: Concordia Publishing House; Philadelphia: Fortress Press, 1955–.

——. *D. Martin Luthers Werke.* Kritische Gesamtausgabe. 73 vols. Edited by J. F. K. Knaake et al. Weimar: Herman Böhlaus Nachfolger, 1883–2009.

Maximus the Confessor. *Maximus Confessor: Selected Writings.* Translated by George C. Berthold. Classics of Western Spirituality. New York: Paulist, 1985.

Plotinus. *The Enneads.* Translated by Stephen MacKenna. London: Faber and Faber, 1962.

——. *Plotini Opera.* Edited by Paul Henry and Hans Rudolf Schwyzer. Paris: Desclée de Brouwer, 1951–1973.

Proclus. *The Elements of Theology.* Edited by E. R. Dodds. Oxford: Clarendon, 1963.

Pseudo-Dionysius. *Pseudo-Dionysius Areopagita: De Coelesti Hierarchia, De Ecclesiastica Hierarchia, De Mystica Theologia, Epistulae.* In *Corpus Dionysiacum*, Volume 2, edited by Günter Heil and Adolf M. Ritter. Patristische Texte und Studien 36. Berlin: De Gruyter, 1991.

——. *Pseudo-Dionysius Areopagita: De Divinis Nominibus.* In *Corpus Dionysiacum*, Volume 1, edited by Beate Regina Suchla. Patristische Texte und Studien 33. Berlin: De Gruyter, 1990.

——. *Pseudo-Dionysius, the Areopagite: The Ecclesiastical Hierarchy.* Translated by Thomas L. Campbell. Washington, DC: University Press of America, 1981.

——. *Pseudo-Dionysius: The Complete Works*. Translated by Colm Luibheid and Paul Rorem. Classics of Western Spirituality. New York: Paulist, 1987.

The Pursuit of Wisdom and Other Works by the Author of the Cloud of Unknowing. Translated and edited by James A. Walsh. Classics of Western Spirituality. New York: Paulist, 1988.

William of Saint-Thierry. *On Contemplating God: Prayer, Meditations*. Cistercian Fathers 3. Kalamazoo, MI: Cistercian Publications, 1977.

——. *The Way to Divine Union: Selected Spiritual Writings*. Edited by M. Basil Pennington. Hyde Park, NY: New City, 1998.

Secondary Texts

Andia, Ysabel de. *Denys l'Aréopagite: Tradition et metamorphoses*. Paris: J. Vrin, 2006.

——. *Henosis: L'union à Dieu chez Denys L'Aréopagite*. Leiden: Brill, 1996.

Arthur, Rosemary A. *Pseudo-Dionysius as Polemicist*. Aldershot: Ashgate, 2008.

Balthasar, Hans Urs von. *The Cosmic Liturgy: The Universe According to Maximus the Confessor*. Translated by Brian E. Daley. San Francisco: Ignatius, 2003.

——. *Elucidations*. Translated by John Riches. London: SPCK, 1975.

——. *Kosmische Liturgie: das Weltbild Maximus' des Bekenners*. 2nd ed. Einsiedeln, Switzerland: Johannes-Verlag, 1961.

——. "Das Scholienwerk des Johannes von Scythopolis." *Scholastik* 15 (1940): 16–38.

Baron, Roger. *Etudes sur Hugues de Saint-Victor*. Paris: Desclée de Brouwer, 1963.

Beierwaltes, W. "Johannes von Skythopolis und Plotin." In *Studia Patristica* 11.2, *Texte und Untersuchungen* 108, 3–7. Berlin: Akademie-Verlag, 1972.

Bell, Theo. *Divus Bernardus: Bernhard von Clairvaux in Martin Luthers Schriften*. Mainz: P. von Zabern, 1993.

Blankenhorn, Bernhard. *The Mystery of Union with God: Dionysian Mysticism in Albert the Great and Thomas Aquinas*. Washington, DC: The Catholic University of America Press, 2015.

Blaumeiser, Hubertus. *Martin Luthers Kreuzestheologie: Schlüssel zu seiner Deutung von Mensch und Wirklichkeit, Eine Untersuchung anhand der Operationes in Psalmos (1519–1521)*. Paderborn: Bonifatius, 1995.

Boissard, Edmond. "Saint Bernard et le Pseudo-Aréopagite." *Recherches de Théologie Ancienne et Médiévale* 26 (1959): 214–63.

Burrows, Mark. "Words that Reach into the Silence: Mystical Languages of Unsaying." In *Minding the Spirit: The Study of Christian Spirituality*, edited by Mark S. Burrows and Elizabeth A. Dreyer, 207–14. Baltimore: Johns Hopkins University Press, 2005.

Cappuyns, Maïeul. *Jean Scot Érigène, sa vie, son oeuvre, sa pensée*. Louvain: Abbaye du Mont César, 1933.

Carabine, Deirdre. "Gregory of Nyssa on the Incomprehensibility of God." In *The Relationship between Neoplatonism and Christianity*, edited by Thomas Finan and Vincent Twomey, 79–99. Dublin: Four Courts, 1992.

Casarella, Peter J. "On the 'Reading Method' in Rorem's *Pseudo-Dionysius*," *The Thomist* 59 (1995): 633-644.

Châtillon, Jean. "Hugues de Saint-Victor critique de Jean Scot." In *Jean Scot Érigène et l'histoire de la philosophie*, edited by Édouard Jeauneau, Goulven Madec, and René Roques, 415–31. Paris: Centre national de la recherché scientifique, 1977.

Coolman, Boyd. "The Medieval Affective Dionysian Tradition." In *Re-Thinking Dionysius the Areopagite*, edited by Sarah Coakley and Charles M. Stang, 85–102. Malden, MA: Wiley Blackwell, 2009. Originally published in *Modern Theology* 24, no. 4 (2008).

Cousins, Ewert. *Bonaventure and the Coincidence of Opposites*. Chicago: Franciscan Herald, 1978.

Curiello, Giocchino. "Pseudo-Dionysius and Damascius: An Impossible Identification." *Dionysius* 31 (2013): 101-116.

Daniélou, Jean. *Platonisme et théologie mystique: essai sur la doctrine spirituelle de saint Grégoire de Nysse*. Paris: Aubier, 1944.

Delaporte, Marianne M. "He Darkens Me with Brightness: The Theology of Pseudo-Dionysius in Hilduin's *Vita* of Saint Denis." *Religion and Theology* 13 (2006): 219–46.

Dondaine, Hyacinthe François. *Le corpus dionysien de l'Université de Paris au XIIIe Siècle*. Rome: Edizioni di Storia e Letteratura, 1953.

Fisher, Jeffrey. "The Theology of Dis/similarity: Negation in Pseudo-Dionysius." *Journal of Religion* 81 (2001): 529–48.

Flusin, Bernard. *Miracle et Histoire dans l'oeuvre de Cyrille de Scythopolis*. Paris: Etudes augustiniennes, 1983.

Forde, Gerhard O. *On Being a Theologian of the Cross: Reflections on Luther's Heidelberg Disputation, 1518*. Grand Rapids, MI: Eerdmans, 1997.

Forte, Bruno. "L'universo dionisiano nel prologo della *Mistica teologia*." *Medioevo* 4 (1978): 1–57.

Froehlich, Karlfried. "Pseudo-Dionysius and the Reformation of the Sixteenth Century." In *Pseudo-Dionysius: The Complete Works*, translated by Colm Luibhéid. New York: Paulist, 1987.

Gersh, Stephen. "Dionysius' *On Divine Names* Revisited: A Structural Analysis." *Dionysius* 28 (2010): 77–96.

Golitzin, Alexander. *Mystagogy: A Monastic Reading of Dionysius Areopagita*. Edited by Bogdan G. Bucur. Collegeville, MN: Liturgical Press, 2013.

Gray, Patrick T. R. *The Defense of Chalcedon in the East (451–553)*. Leiden: Brill, 1979.

Grillmeier, Alois. *Jesus der Christus im Glauben der Kirche*. Vol. 2/2. Freiberg: Herder, 1989.

Harrington, L. Michael. *A Thirteenth-Century Textbook of Medieval Theology at the University of Paris*. Paris: Peeters, 2004.

Hathaway, Ronald F. *Hierarchy and the Definition of Order in the Letters of Pseudo-Dionysius*. The Hague: M. Nijhoff, 1969.

Hayes, Zachary. *The Hidden Center: Spirituality and Speculative Christology in St. Bonaventure*. New York: Paulist, 1981.

Hendrix, Scott H. *Ecclesia in Via*. Leiden: Brill, 1974.

Hollywood, Amy. *The Soul as Virgin Wife*. Notre Dame, IN: University of Notre Dame Press, 1995.

Jantzen, Grace. *Power, Gender, and Christian Mysticism*. Cambridge: Cambridge University Press, 1995.

Knepper, Timothy D. *Negating Negation: Against the Apophatic Abandonment of the Dionysian Corpus*. Eugene, OR: Cascade Books, 2014.

Köhler, Walther. *Luther und die Kirchengeschichte nach seinen Schriften, zunachst bis 1521*. Erlangen: Fr. Junge, 1900.

Kotter, Bonifatius, ed. *Die Schriften des Johannes von Damaskos*. Patristische Texte und Studien 12. Berlin: De Gruyter, 1973.

Lanzetta, Beverly. *Radical Wisdom: A Feminist Mystical Theology*. Minneapolis: Fortress Press, 2005.

Levinas. Emmanuel. "The Trace of the Other." In *Deconstruction in Context: Literature and Philosophy*, edited by Mark C. Taylor, 345–59. Chicago: University of Chicago Press, 1987.

Loewenich, Walther von. *Luthers Theologia Crucis*. Munich: C. Kaiser, 1954.

———. *Luther's Theology of the Cross*. 4th ed. Translated by Herbert J. A. Bouman. Minneapolis: Augsburg, 1976.

Louth, Andrew. *Maximus the Confessor*. London: Routledge, 1996.

Luscombe, David. "The Commentary of Hugh of Saint-Victor on the Celestial Hierarchy." In *Die Dionysius-Rezeption im Mittelalter*, edited by Tzotcho Boiadjiev, Georgi Kapriev, and Andreas Speer, 160–64. Turnholt: Brepols, 2000.

Malysz, Piotr J. "Luther and Dionysius: Beyond Mere Negations." In *Re-Thinking Dionysius the Areopagite*, edited by Sarah Coakley and Charles M. Stang, 149–62. Malden, MA: Wiley-Blackwell, 2009. Originally published in *Modern Theology* 24, no. 4 (2008).

Marion, Jean-Luc. "In the Name, How to Avoid Speaking of 'Negative Theology.'" In *God, the Gift, and Post-Modernism*, edited by John D. Caputo and Michael J. Scanlon., 42-47, 68-70. Bloomington: Indiana University Press, 1999.

Mazzuchi, C. M. "Damascio, autore de Corpus Dionysiacum . . ." *Aevum* 80 (2006): 299–334.

McGinn, Bernard. *The Mystical Thought of Meister Eckhart: The Man from Whom God Hid Nothing.* New York: Crossroad, 2001.

———. *The Presence of God: A History of Western Christian Mysticism.* Vol. 1, *The Foundations of Mysticism*. New York: Crossroad, 1994.

———. "*Vere tu es dues absconditus*: The Hidden God in Luther and Some Mystics." In *Silence and the Word: Negative Theology and Incarnation*, edited by Oliver Davies and Denys Turner, 94–114. Cambridge: Cambridge University Press, 2008.

McGrath, Alister E. *Luther's Theology of the Cross: Martin Luther's Theological Breakthrough*. Oxford: Basil Blackwell, 1985.

Meyendorff, John. *Christ in Eastern Christian Thought*. Washington: Corpus Books, 1989.

———. *A Study of Gregory Palamas*. Translated by George Lawrence. London: Faith Press, 1964.

Moeller, Charles. "Le Chalcédonisme et le néo-chalcédonisme en Orient de 451 à la fin du VIe siècle." In *Das Konzil von Chalkedon: Geschichte und Gegenwart*, edited by Alois Grillmeier and Heinrich Bacht, 1: 666–96. Wurzburg: Echter-Verlag, 1951.

Oberman, Heiko. "*Simul gemitus et raptus*: Luther und die Mystik." In *The Church, Mysticism, Sanctification, and the Natural in Luther's Thought:*

Lectures Presented to the Third International Congress on Luther Research, Järvenpää, Finland, edited by Ivar Asheim, 20–59. Philadelphia: Fortress Press, 1967.

Perczel, Istvan. "The Earliest, Syriac Reception of Dionysius" In *Re-thinking Dionysius the* Areopagite, edited by Sarah Coakley and Charles M. Stang, 27-41. Malden, MA: Wiley-Blackwell, 2009. Originally published in Modern *Theology* 24, no. 4 (2008): 557–71.

Poirel, Dominique. "'Alter Augustinus—der zweite Augustinus': Hugo von Sankt Victor und die Väter der Kirche." In *Väter der Kirche: Ekklesiales Denken von den Anfängen bis in die Neuzeit, Festgabe für Hermann Josef Sieben*, edited by Johannes Arnold, Rainer Berndt, and Ralf M. W. Stammberger, 643–68. Paderborn: F. Schöningh, 2004.

———. "L'ange gothique." In *L'architecture gothique au service de la liturgie*, edited by Agnès Bos and Xavier Dectot, 115–42. Turnhout: Brepols, 2003.

———. "Le 'chant dionysien' du IXe au XIIe siècle." In *Les Historiens et le latin médiéval*, edited by Monique Goullet and Michel Parisse, 151–76. Histoire ancienne et médiévale 63. Paris: Publications de la Sorbonne, 2001.

———. "*Hugo Saxo*: Les origines germaniques de la pensée d'Hugues de Saint Victor." *Francia: Forschungen zur westeuropäischen Geschichte* 33, no. 1 (2006): 163–74.

———. *Livre de la nature et débat trinitaire au XIIe siècle: le De tribus diebus de Hughes de Saint-Victor*. Turnhout: Brepols, 2002.

———. *Des symbole et des anges: Hugues de Saint-Victor et le réveil dionysien du XIIe siècle*. Turnhout: Brepols, 2013.

Posset, Franz. "Bernhard von Clairvauxs Sermone zur Weih-nachts-, Fasten- und Osterzeit als Quelle Martin Luthers." *Lutherjarhbuch* 61 (1994): 93–116.

———. "Saint Bernard of Clairvaux in the Devotion, Theology, and Art of the Sixteenth Century." *Lutheran Quarterly* 11 (1997): 309–52.

Roques, René. *Structures théologiques de la Gnose à Richard de Saint-Victor: Essays et analyses critiques*. Paris: Presse Universitaires de France, 1962.

Rorem, Paul. *Biblical and Liturgical Symbols within the Pseudo-Dionysian Synthesis*. Toronto: Pontifical Institute of Mediaeval Studies, 1984.

———. *Eriugena's Commentary on the Dionysian Celestial Hierarchy*. Toronto: Pontifical Institute of Mediaeval Studies, 2005.

———. *Hugh of St. Victor*. New York: Oxford University Press, 2009.

———. *Pseudo-Dionysius: A Commentary on the Texts and an Introduction to Their Influence*. New York: Oxford University Press, 1993.

Rorem, Paul, and John C. Lamoreaux. "John of Scythopolis on Apollinarian Christology and the Pseudo-Areopagite's True Identity." *Church History* 62 (1993): 469–82.

———. *John of Scythopolis and the Dionysian Corpus: Annotating the Areopagite*. Oxford: Clarendon, 1998.

Saffrey, H. D. "Un lien objectif entre le Pseudo-Denys et Proclus." In *Studia Patristica* 9, *Texte und Untersuchungen* 94, 98–105. Berlin: Akademie-Verlag, 1966.

———. "Nouveaux liens objectifs entre le Pseudo-Denys et Proclus." *Revue des Sciences philosophiques et theologiques* 63 (1979): 3–16.

Schäfer, Christian. *The Philosophy of Dionysius the Areopagite: An Introduction to the Structure and the Content of the Treatise On the Divine Names*. Leiden: Brill, 2006.

Seouh, Jong Won. "Knowledge and Action in Hugh of St. Victor's Commentary on the Dionysian *Celestial Hierarchy*." Ph.D. diss., Princeton Theological Seminary, 2007.

Stang, Charles M. *Apophasis and Pseudonymity in Dionysius the Areopagite: "No Longer I."* Oxford: Oxford University Press, 2012.

Suchla, Beate Regina. "Die sogenannten Maximus-Scholien des Corpus Dionysiacum Areopagiticum." *Nachrichten der Akademie der*

Wissenschaften in Gottingen, I. Philologisch Historische Klasse 3 (1980): 31–66.

———. "Die Überlieferung des Prologs des Johannes von Scythopolis zum griechischen Corpus Dionysiacum Areopagiticum." *Nachrichten der Akademie der Wissenschaften in Gottingen,* I. Philologisch Historische Klasse, 4 (1984): 176–87.

Théry, Gabriel. *Études Dionysiennes.* Vol. 1, *Hilduin, Traducteur de Denys.* Paris: J. Vrin, 1932.

Tigerstedt, E. N. *The Decline and Fall of the Neoplatonic Interpretation of Plato: An Outline and Some Observations.* Commentation es Humanarum Litterarum 52. Helsinki: Societas Scientiarum Fennica, 1974.

Tracy, David. "The Hidden God: The Divine Other of Liberation." *Cross Currents* 46 (Spring 1996): 5–16.

Turner, Denys. "Apophaticism, Idolatry, and the Claims of Reason." In *Silence and the Word: Negative Theology and Incarnation,* edited by Oliver Davies and Denys Turner, 11–34. Cambridge: Cambridge University Press, 2008.

Vanneste, Jean. *Le Mystére de Dieu: Essai sur la structure rationelle de la doctrine mystique du Pseudo-Denys l'Aréopagite.* Paris: De Brouwer, 1959.

Vogelsang, Erich. "Luther und die Mystik." *Luther-Jahrbuch* 19 (1937): 32–54.

Weisweiler, Heinrich. "Die Pseudo-Dionysiuskommentare 'In Coelestem Hierarchiam' des Skotus Eriugena und Hugos von St. Viktor." *Recherches de théologie ancienne et médiévale* 19 (1952): 26–47.

Westhelle, Vitor. *The Scandalous God: The Use and Abuse of the Cross.* Minneapolis: Fortress Press, 2006.

Zinn, Grover A., Jr. "*De gradibus ascensionum*: The Stages of Contemplative Ascent in Two Treatises on Noah's Ark by Hugh of St. Victor." In *Studies in Medieval Culture,* edited by John R. Sommerfeldt, 5:61–79. Kalamazoo, MI: Medieval Institute, 1975.

———. "Texts within Texts: The Song of Songs in the Exegesis of Gregory the Great and Hugh of St. Victor." In *Studia Patristica* 25, 209–15. Leuven: Peeters, 1993.

Zur Mühlen, Karl-Heinz. *Nos Extra Nos: Luthers Theologie zwischen Mystik und Scholastik.* Tubingen: J. C. B. Mohr, 1972.

Index of Names